Mometrix
TEST PREPARATION

M000308800

MEGA

Elementary Education Multi-Content (073-074)

Secrets Study Guide

Part 3 of 3

DEAR FUTURE EXAM SUCCESS STORY

First of all, **THANK YOU** for purchasing Mometrix study materials!

Second, congratulations! You are one of the few determined test-takers who are committed to doing whatever it takes to excel on your exam. **You have come to the right place.** We developed these study materials with one goal in mind: to deliver you the information you need in a format that's concise and easy to use.

In addition to optimizing your guide for the content of the test, we've outlined our recommended steps for breaking down the preparation process into small, attainable goals so you can make sure you stay on track.

We've also analyzed the entire test-taking process, identifying the most common pitfalls and showing how you can overcome them and be ready for any curveball the test throws you.

Standardized testing is one of the biggest obstacles on your road to success, which only increases the importance of doing well in the high-pressure, high-stakes environment of test day. Your results on this test could have a significant impact on your future, and this guide provides the information and practical advice to help you achieve your full potential on test day.

Your success is our success

We would love to hear from you! If you would like to share the story of your exam success or if you have any questions or comments in regard to our products, please contact us at **800-673-8175** or **support@mometrix.com**.

Thanks again for your business and we wish you continued success!

Sincerely,
The Mometrix Test Preparation Team

Need more help? Check out our flashcards at:
http://mometrixflashcards.com/MEGA

Written and edited by the Mometrix Exam Secrets Test Prep Team
Printed in the United States of America

TABLE OF CONTENTS

English Language Arts

Transform passive reading into active learning! After immersing yourself in this chapter, put your comprehension to the test by taking a quiz. The insights you gained will stay with you longer this way. Scan the QR code to go directly to the chapter quiz interface for this study guide. If you're using a computer, simply visit the bonus page at **mometrix.com/bonus948/megaeemc073074** and click the Chapter Quizzes link.

Setting, Mood, Tone, and Perspective in Literary Texts

Setting and Time Frame

A literary text has both a setting and time frame. A **setting** is the place in which the story as a whole is set. The **time frame** is the period in which the story is set. This may refer to the historical period the story takes place in or if the story takes place over a single day. Both setting and time frame are relevant to a text's meaning because they help the reader place the story in time and space. An author uses setting and time frame to anchor a text, create a mood, and enhance its meaning. This helps a reader understand why a character acts the way he does, or why certain events in the story are important. The setting impacts the **plot** and character **motivations**, while the time frame helps place the story in **chronological context**.

Example

Read the following excerpt from The Adventures of Huckleberry Finn by Mark Twain and analyze the relevance of setting to the text's meaning:

> We said there warn't no home like a raft, after all. Other places do seem so cramped up and smothery, but a raft don't. You feel mighty free and easy and comfortable on a raft.

This excerpt from *The Adventures of Huckleberry Finn* by Mark Twain reveals information about the **setting** of the book. By understanding that the main character, Huckleberry Finn, lives on a raft, the reader can place the story on a river, in this case, the Mississippi River in the South before the Civil War. The information about the setting also gives the reader clues about the **character** of Huck Finn: he clearly values independence and freedom, and he likes the outdoors. The information about the setting in the quote helps the reader to better understand the rest of the text.

Syntax and Word Choice

Authors use words and **syntax**, or sentence structure, to make their texts unique, convey their own writing style, and sometimes to make a point or emphasis. They know that word choice and syntax contribute to the reader's understanding of the text as well as to the tone and mood of a text.

Review Video: What is Syntax?
Visit mometrix.com/academy and enter code: 242280

Mood and Tone

Mood is a story's atmosphere, or the feelings the reader gets from reading it. The way authors set the mood in writing is comparable to the way filmmakers use music to set the mood in movies. Instead of music, though, writers judiciously select descriptive words to evoke certain **moods**. The mood of a work may convey joy, anger, bitterness, hope, gloom, fear, apprehension, or any other emotion the author wants the reader to feel. In addition to vocabulary choices, authors also use figurative expressions, particular sentence structures, and choices of diction that project and reinforce the moods they want to create. Whereas mood is the reader's emotions evoked by reading what is written, **tone** is the emotions and attitudes of the writer that she or he expresses in the writing. Authors use the same literary techniques to establish tone as they do to establish mood. An author may use a humorous tone, an angry or sad tone, a sentimental or unsentimental tone, or something else entirely.

Mood and Tone in The Great Gatsby

To understand the difference between mood and tone, look at this excerpt from F. Scott Fitzgerald's *The Great Gatsby*. In this passage, Nick Caraway, the novel's narrator, is describing his affordable house, which sits in a neighborhood full of expensive mansions.

> "I lived at West Egg, the—well the less fashionable of the two, though this is a most superficial tag to express the bizarre and not a little sinister contrast between them. My house was at the very tip of the egg, only fifty yard from the Sound, and squeezed between two huge places that rented for twelve or fifteen thousand a season ... My own house was an eyesore, but it was a small eyesore, and it had been overlooked, so I had a view of the water, a partial view of my neighbor's lawn, and the consoling proximity of millionaires—all for eighty dollars a month."

In this description, the mood created for the reader does not match the tone created through the narrator. The mood in this passage is one of dissatisfaction and inferiority. Nick compares his home to his neighbors', saying he lives in the "less fashionable" neighborhood and that his house is "overlooked," an "eyesore," and "squeezed between two huge" mansions. He also adds that his placement allows him the "consoling proximity of millionaires." A literal reading of these details leads the reader to have negative feelings toward Nick's house and his economic inferiority to his neighbors, creating the mood.

However, Fitzgerald also conveys an opposing attitude, or tone, through Nick's description. Nick calls the distinction between the neighborhoods "superficial," showing a suspicion of the value suggested by the neighborhoods' titles, properties, and residents. Nick also undermines his critique of his own home by calling it "a small eyesore" and claiming it has "been overlooked." However, he follows these statements with a description of his surroundings, claiming that he has "a view of the water" and can see some of his wealthy neighbor's property from his home, and a comparison between the properties' rent. While the mental image created for the reader depicts a small house shoved between looming mansions, the tone suggests that Nick enjoys these qualities about his home, or at least finds it charming. He acknowledges its shortcomings, but includes the benefits of his home's unassuming appearance.

Review Video: Style, Tone, and Mood
Visit mometrix.com/academy and enter code: 416961

Point of View

Another element that impacts a text is the author's point of view. The **point of view** of a text is the perspective from which a passage is told. An author will always have a point of view about a story before he or she draws up a plot line. The author will know what events they want to take place, how they want the characters to interact, and how they want the story to resolve. An author will also have an opinion on the topic or series of events which is presented in the story that is based on their prior experience and beliefs.

The two main points of view that authors use, especially in a work of fiction, are first person and third person. If the narrator of the story is also the main character, or *protagonist*, the text is written in first-person point of view. In first person, the author writes from the perspective of *I*. Third-person point of view is probably the most common that authors use in their passages. Using third person, authors refer to each character by using *he* or *she*. In third-person omniscient, the narrator is not a character in the story and tells the story of all of the characters at the same time.

Review Video: Point of View
Visit mometrix.com/academy and enter code: 383336

First-Person Narration

First-person narratives let narrators express inner feelings and thoughts, especially when the narrator is the protagonist as Lemuel Gulliver is in Jonathan Swift's *Gulliver's Travels.* The narrator may be a close friend of the protagonist, like Dr. Watson in Sir Arthur Conan Doyle's *Sherlock Holmes.* Or, the narrator can be less involved with the main characters and plot, like Nick Carraway in F. Scott Fitzgerald's *The Great Gatsby.* When a narrator reports others' narratives, she or he is a "**frame narrator**," like the nameless narrator of Joseph Conrad's *Heart of Darkness* or Mr. Lockwood in Emily Brontë's *Wuthering Heights.* **First-person plural** is unusual but can be effective. Isaac Asimov's *I, Robot*, William Faulkner's *A Rose for Emily*, Maxim Gorky's *Twenty-Six Men and a Girl*, and Jeffrey Eugenides' *The Virgin Suicides* all use first-person plural narration. Author Kurt Vonnegut is the first-person narrator in his semi-autobiographical novel *Timequake.* Also unusual, but effective, is a **first-person omniscient** (rather than the more common third-person omniscient) narrator, like Death in Markus Zusak's *The Book Thief* and the ghost in Alice Sebold's *The Lovely Bones.*

Second-Person Narration

While **second-person** address is very commonplace in popular song lyrics, it is the least used form of narrative voice in literary works. Popular serial books of the 1980s like *Fighting Fantasy* or *Choose Your Own Adventure* employed second-person narratives. In some cases, a narrative combines both second-person and first-person voices, using the pronouns *you* and *I*. This can draw readers into the story, and it can also enable the authors to compare directly "your" and "my" feelings, thoughts, and actions. When the narrator is also a character in the story, as in Edgar Allan Poe's short story "The Tell-Tale Heart" or Jay McInerney's novel *Bright Lights, Big City,* the narrative is better defined as first-person despite it also addressing "you."

Third-Person Narration

Narration in the third person is the most prevalent type, as it allows authors the most flexibility. It is so common that readers simply assume without needing to be informed that the narrator is not a character in the story, or involved in its events. **Third-person singular** is used more frequently than **third-person plural**, though some authors have also effectively used plural. However, both singular and plural are most often included in stories according to which characters are being described. The third-person narrator may be either objective or subjective, and either omniscient or limited. **Objective third-person** narration does not include what the characters described are thinking or feeling, while **subjective third-person** narration does. The **third-person omniscient** narrator knows everything about all characters, including their thoughts and emotions, and all related places, times, and events. However, the **third-person limited** narrator may know everything about a particular character, but is limited to that character. In other words, the narrator cannot speak about anything that character does not know.

Alternating-Person Narration

Although authors more commonly write stories from one point of view, there are also instances wherein they alternate the narrative voice within the same book. For example, they may sometimes use an omniscient third-person narrator and a more intimate first-person narrator at other times. In J. K. Rowling's series of *Harry Potter* novels, she often writes in a third-person limited narrative, but sometimes changes to narration by characters other than the protagonist. George R. R. Martin's series *A Song of Ice and Fire* changes the point of view to coincide with divisions between chapters. The same technique is used by Erin Hunter (a pseudonym for several authors of the *Warriors, Seekers,* and *Survivors* book series). Authors using first-person narrative sometimes switch to third-person to describe significant action scenes, especially those where the narrator was absent or uninvolved, as Barbara Kingsolver does in her novel *The Poisonwood Bible.*

Historical and Social Context

Fiction that is heavily influenced by a historical or social context cannot be comprehended as the author intended if the reader does not keep this context in mind. Many important elements of the text will be influenced by any context, including symbols, allusions, settings, and plot events. These contexts, as well as the identity of the work's author, can help to inform the reader about the author's concerns and intended meanings. For example, George Orwell published his novel *1984* in the year 1949, soon after the end of World War II. At that time, following the defeat of the Nazis, the Cold War began between the Western Allied nations and the Eastern Soviet Communists. People were therefore concerned about the conflict between the freedoms afforded by Western democracies versus the oppression represented by Communism. Orwell had also previously fought in the Spanish Civil War against a Spanish regime that he and his fellows viewed as oppressive. From this information, readers can infer that Orwell was concerned about oppression by totalitarian governments. This informs *1984*'s story of Winston Smith's rebellion against the oppressive "Big Brother" government, of the fictional dictatorial state of Oceania, and his capture, torture, and ultimate conversion by that government. Some literary theories also seek to use historical and social contexts to reveal deeper meanings and implications in a text.

Plot and Story Structure

Theme

The **theme** of a passage is what the reader learns from the text or the passage. It is the lesson or **moral** contained in the passage. It also is a unifying idea that is used throughout the text; it can take the form of a common setting, idea, symbol, design, or recurring event. A passage can have two or more themes that convey its overall idea. The theme or themes of a passage are often based on **universal themes**. They can frequently be expressed using well-known sayings about life, society, or human nature, such as "Hard work pays off" or "Good triumphs over evil." Themes are not usually stated **explicitly**. The reader must figure them out by carefully reading the passage. Themes are often the reason why passages are written; they give a passage unity and meaning. Themes are created through **plot development**. The events of a story help shape the themes of a passage.

EXAMPLE

Explain why "Take care of what you care about" accurately describes the theme of the following excerpt.

> Luca collected baseball cards, but he wasn't very careful with them. He left them around the house. His dog liked to chew. One day, Luca and his friend Bart were looking at his collection. Then they went outside. When Luca got home, he saw his dog chewing on his cards. They were ruined.

This excerpt tells the story of a boy who is careless with his baseball cards and leaves them lying around. His dog ends up chewing them and ruining them. The lesson is that if you care about something, you need to take care of it. This is the theme, or point, of the story. Some stories have more than one theme, but this is not really true of this excerpt. The reader needs to figure out the theme based on what happens in the story. Sometimes, as in the case of fables, the theme is stated directly in the text. However, this is not usually the case.

Review Video: Themes in Literature
Visit mometrix.com/academy and enter code: 732074

PLOT AND STORY STRUCTURE

The **plot** includes the events that happen in a story and the order in which they are told to the reader. There are several types of plot structures, as stories can be told in many ways. The most common plot structure is the chronological plot, which presents the events to the reader in the same order they occur for the characters in the story. Chronological plots usually have five main parts, the **exposition**, **rising action**, the **climax**, **falling action**, and the **resolution**. This type of plot structure guides the reader through the story's events as the characters experience them and is the easiest structure to understand and identify. While this is the most common plot structure, many stories are nonlinear, which means the plot does not sequence events in the same order the characters experience them. Such stories might include elements like flashbacks that cause the story to be nonlinear.

Review Video: How to Make a Story Map
Visit mometrix.com/academy and enter code: 261719

EXPOSITION

The **exposition** is at the beginning of the story and generally takes place before the rising action begins. The purpose of the exposition is to give the reader context for the story, which the author may do by introducing one or more characters, describing the setting or world, or explaining the events leading up to the point where the story begins. The exposition may still include events that contribute to the plot, but the **rising action** and main conflict of the story are not part of the exposition. Some narratives skip the exposition and begin the story with the beginning of the rising action, which causes the reader to learn the context as the story intensifies.

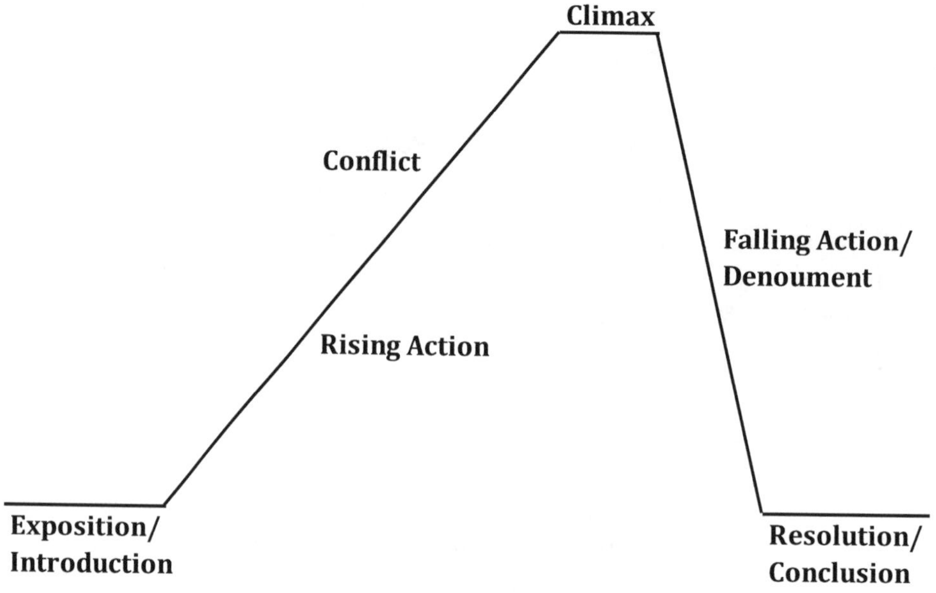

Review Video: Plot line Definition
Visit mometrix.com/academy and enter code: 944011

Conflict

A **conflict** is a problem to be solved. Literary plots typically include one conflict or more. Characters' attempts to resolve conflicts drive the narrative's forward movement. **Conflict resolution** is often the protagonist's primary occupation. Physical conflicts like exploring, wars, and escapes tend to make plots most suspenseful and exciting. Emotional, mental, or moral conflicts tend to make stories more personally gratifying or rewarding for many audiences. Conflicts can be external or internal. A major type of internal conflict is some inner personal battle, or **man versus self**. Major types of external conflicts include **man versus nature**, **man versus man**, and **man versus society**. Readers can identify conflicts in literary plots by identifying the protagonist and antagonist and asking why they conflict, what events develop the conflict, where the climax occurs, and how they identify with the characters.

Read the following paragraph and discuss the type of conflict present:

> Timothy was shocked out of sleep by the appearance of a bear just outside his tent. After panicking for a moment, he remembered some advice he had read in preparation for this trip: he should make noise so the bear would not be startled. As Timothy started to hum and sing, the bear wandered away.

There are three main types of conflict in literature: **man versus man**, **man versus nature**, and **man versus self**. This paragraph is an example of man versus nature. Timothy is in conflict with the bear. Even though no physical conflict like an attack exists, Timothy is pitted against the bear.

Timothy uses his knowledge to "defeat" the bear and keep himself safe. The solution to the conflict is that Timothy makes noise, the bear wanders away, and Timothy is safe.

Review Video: Conflict
Visit mometrix.com/academy and enter code: 559550

Review Video: Determining Relationships in a Story
Visit mometrix.com/academy and enter code: 929925

Rising Action

The **rising action** is the part of the story where conflict **intensifies**. The rising action begins with an event that prompts the main conflict of the story. This may also be called the **inciting incident**. The main conflict generally occurs between the protagonist and an antagonist, but this is not the only type of conflict that may occur in a narrative. After this event, the protagonist works to resolve the main conflict by preparing for an altercation, pursuing a goal, fleeing an antagonist, or doing some other action that will end the conflict. The rising action is composed of several additional events that increase the story's tension. Most often, other developments will occur alongside the growth of the main conflict, such as character development or the development of minor conflicts. The rising action ends with the **climax**, which is the point of highest tension in the story.

Climax

The **climax** is the event in the narrative that marks the height of the story's conflict or tension. The event that takes place at the story's climax will end the rising action and bring about the results of the main conflict. If the conflict was between a good protagonist and an evil antagonist, the climax may be a final battle between the two characters. If the conflict is an adventurer looking for heavily guarded treasure, the climax may be the adventurer's encounter with the final obstacle that protects the treasure. The climax may be made of multiple scenes, but can usually be summarized as one event. Once the conflict and climax are complete, the **falling action** begins.

Falling Action

The **falling action** shows what happens in the story between the climax and the resolution. The falling action often composes a much smaller portion of the story than the rising action does. While the climax includes the end of the main conflict, the falling action may show the results of any minor conflicts in the story. For example, if the protagonist encountered a troll on the way to find some treasure, and the troll demanded the protagonist share the treasure after retrieving it, the falling action would include the protagonist returning to share the treasure with the troll. Similarly, any unexplained major events are usually made clear during the falling action. Once all significant elements of the story are resolved or addressed, the story's resolution will occur. The **resolution** is the end of the story, which shows the final result of the plot's events and shows what life is like for the main characters once they are no longer experiencing the story's conflicts.

Resolution

The way the conflict is **resolved** depends on the type of conflict. The plot of any book starts with the lead up to the conflict, then the conflict itself, and finally the solution, or **resolution**, to the conflict. In **man versus man** conflicts, the conflict is often resolved by two parties coming to some sort of agreement or by one party triumphing over the other party. In **man versus nature** conflicts, the conflict is often resolved by man coming to some realization about some aspect of nature. In

man versus self conflicts, the conflict is often resolved by the character growing or coming to an understanding about part of himself.

CHARACTER DEVELOPMENT

When depicting characters or figures in a written text, authors generally use actions, dialogue, and descriptions as characterization techniques. Characterization can occur in both fiction and nonfiction and is used to show a character or figure's personality, demeanor, and thoughts. This helps create a more engaging experience for the reader by providing a more concrete picture of a character or figure's tendencies and features. Characterizations also gives authors the opportunity to integrate elements such as dialects, activities, attire, and attitudes into their writing.

To understand the meaning of a story, it is vital to understand the characters as the author describes them. We can look for contradictions in what a character thinks, says, and does. We can notice whether the author's observations about a character differ from what other characters in the story say about that character. A character may be dynamic, meaning they change significantly during the story, or static, meaning they remain the same from beginning to end. Characters may be two-dimensional, not fully developed, or may be well developed with characteristics that stand out vividly. Characters may also symbolize universal properties. Additionally, readers can compare and contrast characters to analyze how each one developed.

A well-known example of character development can be found in Charles Dickens's *Great Expectations*. The novel's main character, Pip, is introduced as a young boy, and he is depicted as innocent, kind, and humble. However, as Pip grows up and is confronted with the social hierarchy of Victorian England, he becomes arrogant and rejects his loved ones in pursuit of his own social advancement. Once he achieves his social goals, he realizes the merits of his former lifestyle, and lives with the wisdom he gained in both environments and life stages. Dickens shows Pip's ever-changing character through his interactions with others and his inner thoughts, which evolve as his personal values and personality shift.

Review Video: Character Changes
Visit mometrix.com/academy and enter code: 408719

DIALOGUE

Effectively written dialogue serves at least one, but usually several, purposes. It advances the story and moves the plot, develops the characters, sheds light on the work's theme or meaning, and can, often subtly, account for the passage of time not otherwise indicated. It can alter the direction that the plot is taking, typically by introducing some new conflict or changing existing ones. **Dialogue** can establish a work's narrative voice and the characters' voices and set the tone of the story or of particular characters. When fictional characters display enlightenment or realization, dialogue can give readers an understanding of what those characters have discovered and how. Dialogue can illuminate the motivations and wishes of the story's characters. By using consistent thoughts and syntax, dialogue can support character development. Skillfully created, it can also represent real-life speech rhythms in written form. Via conflicts and ensuing action, dialogue also provides drama.

DIALOGUE IN FICTION

In fictional works, effectively written dialogue does more than just break up or interrupt sections of narrative. While **dialogue** may supply exposition for readers, it must nonetheless be believable. Dialogue should be dynamic, not static, and it should not resemble regular prose. Authors should not use dialogue to write clever similes or metaphors, or to inject their own opinions. Nor should they use dialogue at all when narrative would be better. Most importantly, dialogue should not slow the plot movement. Dialogue must seem natural, which means careful construction of phrases rather than actually duplicating natural speech, which does not necessarily translate well to the written word. Finally, all dialogue must be pertinent to the story, rather than just added conversation.

Figurative Language and Literary Devices

Literary Analysis

The best literary analysis shows special insight into at least one important aspect of a text. When analyzing literary texts, it can be difficult to find a starting place. Many texts can be analyzed several different ways, often leaving an overwhelming number of options for writers to consider. However, narrowing the focus to a particular element of literature can be helpful when preparing to analyze a text. Symbolism, themes, and motifs are common starting points for literary analysis. These three methods of analysis can lead to a holistic analysis of a text, since they involve elements that are often distributed throughout the text. However, not all texts feature these elements in a way that facilitates a strong analysis, if they are present at all. It is also common to focus on character or plot development for analysis. These elements are compatible with theme, symbolism, and allusion. Setting and imagery, figurative language, and any external contexts can also contribute to analysis or complement one of these other elements. The application of a critical, or literary, theory to a text can also provide a thorough and strong analysis.

Literal and Figurative Meaning

When language is used **literally**, the words mean exactly what they say and nothing more. When language is used **figuratively**, the words mean something beyond their literal meaning. For example, "The weeping willow tree has long, trailing branches and leaves" is a literal description. But "The weeping willow tree looks as if it is bending over and crying" is a figurative description—specifically, a **simile** or stated comparison. Another figurative language form is **metaphor**, or an implied comparison. A good example is the metaphor of a city, state, or city-state as a ship, and its governance as sailing that ship. Ancient Greek lyrical poet Alcaeus is credited with first using this metaphor, and ancient Greek tragedian Aeschylus then used it in *Seven Against Thebes,* and then Plato used it in the *Republic.*

Figures of Speech

A **figure of speech** is a verbal expression whose meaning is figurative rather than literal. For example, the phrase "butterflies in the stomach" does not refer to actual butterflies in a person's stomach. It is a metaphor representing the fluttery feelings experienced when a person is nervous or excited—or when one "falls in love," which does not mean physically falling. "Hitting a sales target" does not mean physically hitting a target with arrows as in archery; it is a metaphor for meeting a sales quota. "Climbing the ladder of success" metaphorically likens advancing in one's career to ascending ladder rungs. Similes, such as "light as a feather" (meaning very light, not a feather's actual weight), and hyperbole, like "I'm starving/freezing/roasting," are also figures of speech. Figures of speech are often used and crafted for emphasis, freshness of expression, or clarity.

Review Video: Figures of Speech
Visit mometrix.com/academy and enter code: 111295

Figurative Language

Figurative language extends past the literal meanings of words. It offers readers new insight into the people, things, events, and subjects covered in a work of literature. Figurative language also enables readers to feel they are sharing the authors' experiences. It can stimulate the reader's senses, make comparisons that readers find intriguing or even startling, and enable readers to view the world in different ways. When looking for figurative language, it is important to consider the context of the sentence or situation. Phrases that appear out of place or make little sense when read literally are likely instances of figurative language. Once figurative language has been recognized, context is also important to determining the type of figurative language being used and its function. For example, when a comparison is being made, a metaphor or simile is likely being used. This means the comparison may emphasize or create irony through the things being compared. Seven specific types of figurative language include: alliteration, onomatopoeia, personification, imagery, similes, metaphors, and hyperbole.

> **Review Video: Figurative Language**
> Visit mometrix.com/academy and enter code: 584902

Alliteration and Onomatopoeia

Alliteration describes a series of words beginning with the same sounds. **Onomatopoeia** uses words imitating the sounds of things they name or describe. For example, in his poem "Come Down, O Maid," Alfred Tennyson writes of "The moan of doves in immemorial elms, / And murmuring of innumerable bees." The word "moan" sounds like some sounds doves make, "murmuring" represents the sounds of bees buzzing. Onomatopoeia also includes words that are simply meant to represent sounds, such as "meow," "kaboom," and "whoosh."

> **Review Video: Alliterations Are All Around**
> Visit mometrix.com/academy and enter code: 462837

Personification

Another type of figurative language is **personification**. This is describing a non-human thing, like an animal or an object, as if it were human. The general intent of personification is to describe things in a manner that will be comprehensible to readers. When an author states that a tree *groans* in the wind, he or she does not mean that the tree is emitting a low, pained sound from a mouth. Instead, the author means that the tree is making a noise similar to a human groan. Of course, this personification establishes a tone of sadness or suffering. A different tone would be established if the author said that the tree was *swaying* or *dancing*. Alfred Tennyson's poem "The Eagle" uses all of these types of figurative language: "He clasps the crag with crooked hands." Tennyson used alliteration, repeating /k/ and /kr/ sounds. These hard-sounding consonants reinforce the imagery, giving visual and tactile impressions of the eagle.

> **Review Video: Personification**
> Visit mometrix.com/academy and enter code: 260066

Similes and Metaphors

Similes are stated comparisons using "like" or "as." Similes can be used to stimulate readers' imaginations and appeal to their senses. Because a simile includes *like* or *as,* the device creates more space between the description and the thing being described than a metaphor does. If an author says that *a house was like a shoebox*, then the tone is different than the author saying that the house *was* a shoebox. Authors will choose between a metaphor and a simile depending on their intended tone.

Similes also help compare fictional characters to well-known objects or experiences, so the reader can better relate to them. William Wordsworth's poem about "Daffodils" begins, "I wandered lonely as a cloud." This simile compares his loneliness to that of a cloud. It is also personification, giving a cloud the human quality loneliness. In his novel *Lord Jim* (1900), Joseph Conrad writes in Chapter 33, "I would have given anything for the power to soothe her frail soul, tormenting itself in its invincible ignorance like a small bird beating about the cruel wires of a cage." Conrad uses the word "like" to compare the girl's soul to a small bird. His description of the bird beating at the cage shows the similar helplessness of the girl's soul to gain freedom.

Review Video: Similes
Visit mometrix.com/academy and enter code: 642949

A **metaphor** is a type of figurative language in which the writer equates something with another thing that is not particularly similar, instead of using *like* or *as*. For instance, *the bird was an arrow arcing through the sky*. In this sentence, the arrow is serving as a metaphor for the bird. The point of a metaphor is to encourage the reader to consider the item being described in a *different way*. Let's continue with this metaphor for a flying bird. You are asked to envision the bird's flight as being similar to the arc of an arrow. So, you imagine the flight to be swift and bending. Metaphors are a way for the author to describe an item *without being direct and obvious*. This literary device is a lyrical and suggestive way of providing information. Note that the reference for a metaphor will not always be mentioned explicitly by the author. Consider the following description of a forest in winter: *Swaying skeletons reached for the sky and groaned as the wind blew through them.* In this example, the author is using *skeletons* as a metaphor for leafless trees. This metaphor creates a spooky tone while inspiring the reader's imagination.

LITERARY EXAMPLES OF METAPHOR

A **metaphor** is an implied comparison, i.e., it compares something to something else without using "like", "as", or other comparative words. For example, in "The Tyger" (1794), William Blake writes, "Tyger Tyger, burning bright, / In the forests of the night." Blake compares the tiger to a flame not by saying it is like a fire, but by simply describing it as "burning." Henry Wadsworth Longfellow's poem "O Ship of State" (1850) uses an extended metaphor by referring consistently throughout the entire poem to the state, union, or republic as a seagoing vessel, referring to its keel, mast, sail, rope, anchors, and to its braving waves, rocks, gale, tempest, and "false lights on the shore." Within the extended metaphor, Wordsworth uses a specific metaphor: "the anchors of thy hope!"

TED HUGHES' ANIMAL METAPHORS

Ted Hughes frequently used animal metaphors in his poetry. In "The Thought Fox," a model of concise, structured beauty, Hughes characterizes the poet's creative process with succinct, striking imagery of an idea entering his head like a wild fox. Repeating "loneliness" in the first two stanzas emphasizes the poet's lonely work: "Something else is alive / Beside the clock's loneliness." He treats an idea's arrival as separate from himself. Three stanzas detail in vivid images a fox's approach from the outside winter forest at starless midnight—its nose, "Cold, delicately" touching twigs and leaves; "neat" paw prints in snow; "bold" body; brilliant green eyes; and self-contained, focused progress—"Till, with a sudden sharp hot stink of fox," he metaphorically depicts poetic inspiration as the fox's physical entry into "the dark hole of the head." Hughes ends by summarizing his vision of a poet as an interior, passive idea recipient, with the outside world unchanged: "The window is starless still; the clock ticks, / The page is printed."

Review Video: Metaphors in Writing
Visit mometrix.com/academy and enter code: 133295

Metonymy

Metonymy is naming one thing with words or phrases of a closely related thing. This is similar to metaphor. However, the comparison has a close connection, unlike metaphor. An example of metonymy is to call the news media *the press*. Of course, *the press* is the machine that prints newspapers. Metonymy is a way of naming something without using the same name constantly.

Synecdoche

Synecdoche points to the whole by naming one of the parts. An example of synecdoche would be calling a construction worker a *hard hat*. Like metonymy, synecdoche is an easy way of naming something without having to overuse a name. The device allows writers to highlight pieces of the thing being described. For example, referring to businessmen as *suits* suggests professionalism and unity.

Hyperbole

Hyperbole is excessive exaggeration used for humor or emphasis rather than for literal meaning. For example, in *To Kill a Mockingbird*, Harper Lee wrote, "People moved slowly then. There was no hurry, for there was nowhere to go, nothing to buy and no money to buy it with, nothing to see outside the boundaries of Maycomb County." This was not literally true; Lee exaggerates the scarcity of these things for emphasis. In "Old Times on the Mississippi," Mark Twain wrote, "I... could have hung my hat on my eyes, they stuck out so far." This is not literal, but makes his description vivid and funny. In his poem "As I Walked Out One Evening", W. H. Auden wrote, "I'll love you, dear, I'll love you / Till China and Africa meet, / And the river jumps over the mountain / And the salmon sing in the street." He used things not literally possible to emphasize the duration of his love.

Understatement

Understatement is the opposite of hyperbole. This device discounts or downplays something. Think about someone who climbs Mount Everest. Then, they say that the journey was *a little stroll*. As with other types of figurative language, understatement has a range of uses. The device may show self-defeat or modesty as in the Mount Everest example. However, some may think of understatement as false modesty (i.e., an attempt to bring attention to you or a situation). For example, a woman is praised on her diamond engagement ring. The woman says, *Oh, this little thing?* Her understatement might be heard as stuck-up or unfeeling.

Review Video: Hyperbole and Understatement
Visit mometrix.com/academy and enter code: 308470

Literary Irony

In literature, irony demonstrates the opposite of what is said or done. The three types of irony are **verbal irony**, **situational irony**, and **dramatic irony**. Verbal irony uses words opposite to the meaning. Sarcasm may use verbal irony. One common example is describing something that is confusing as "clear as mud." For example, in his 1986 movie *Hannah and Her Sisters,* author, director, and actor Woody Allen says to his character's date, "I had a great evening; it was like the Nuremburg Trials." Notice these employ similes. In situational irony, what happens contrasts with what was expected. O. Henry's short story *The Gift of the Magi* uses situational irony: a husband and wife each sacrifice their most prized possession to buy each other a Christmas present. The irony is that she sells her long hair to buy him a watch fob, while he sells his heirloom pocket-watch to buy her the jeweled combs for her hair she had long wanted; in the end, neither of them can use their gifts. In dramatic irony, narrative informs audiences of more than its characters know. For example, in *Romeo and Juliet,* the audience is made aware that Juliet is only asleep, while Romeo believes her to be dead, which then leads to Romeo's death.

Review Video: What is the Definition of Irony?
Visit mometrix.com/academy and enter code: 374204

IDIOMS

Idioms create comparisons, and often take the form of similes or metaphors. Idioms are always phrases and are understood to have a meaning that is different from its individual words' literal meaning. For example, "break a leg" is a common idiom that is used to wish someone luck or tell them to perform well. Literally, the phrase "break a leg" means to injure a person's leg, but the phrase takes on a different meaning when used as an idiom. Another example is "call it a day," which means to temporarily stop working on a task, or find a stopping point, rather than literally referring to something as "a day." Many idioms are associated with a region or group. For example, an idiom commonly used in the American South is "'til the cows come home." This phrase is often used to indicate that something will take or may last for a very long time, but not that it will literally last until the cows return to where they reside.

ALLUSION

An allusion is an uncited but recognizable reference to something else. Authors use language to make allusions to places, events, artwork, and other books in order to make their own text richer. For example, an author may allude to a very important text in order to make his own text seem more important. Martin Luther King, Jr. started his "I Have a Dream" speech by saying "Five score years ago..." This is a clear allusion to President Abraham Lincoln's "Gettysburg Address" and served to remind people of the significance of the event. An author may allude to a place to ground his text or make a cultural reference to make readers feel included. There are many reasons that authors make allusions.

Review Video: Allusions
Visit mometrix.com/academy and enter code: 294065

COMIC RELIEF

Comic relief is the use of comedy by an author to break up a dramatic or tragic scene and infuse it with a bit of **lightheartedness**. In William Shakespeare's *Hamlet*, two gravediggers digging the grave for Ophelia share a joke while they work. The death and burial of Ophelia are tragic moments that directly follow each other. Shakespeare uses an instance of comedy to break up the tragedy and give his audience a bit of a break from the tragic drama. Authors sometimes use comic relief so that their work will be less depressing; other times they use it to create irony or contrast between the darkness of the situation and the lightness of the joke. Often, authors will use comedy to parallel what is happening in the tragic scenes.

Review Video: What is Comic Relief?
Visit mometrix.com/academy and enter code: 779604

FORESHADOWING

Foreshadowing is a device authors use to give readers **hints** about events that will take place later in a story. Foreshadowing most often takes place through a character's dialogue or actions. Sometimes the character will know what is going to happen and will purposefully allude to future events. For example, consider a protagonist who is about to embark on a journey through the woods. Just before the protagonist begins the trip, another character says, "Be careful, you never know what could be out in those woods!" This alerts the reader that the woods may be dangerous and prompts the reader to expect something to attack the protagonist in the woods. This is an example of foreshadowing through warning. Alternatively, a character may unknowingly foreshadow later events. For example, consider a story where a brother and sister run through their house and knock over a vase and break it. The brother says, "Don't worry, we'll clean it up! Mom will never know!" However, the reader knows that their mother will most likely find out what they have done, so the reader expects the siblings to later get in trouble for running, breaking the vase, and hiding it from their mother.

SYMBOLISM

Symbolism describes an author's use of a **symbol**, an element of the story that **represents** something else. Symbols can impact stories in many ways, including deepening the meaning of a story or its elements, comparing a story to another work, or foreshadowing later events in a story. Symbols can be objects, characters, colors, numbers, or anything else the author establishes as a symbol. Symbols can be clearly established through direct comparison or repetition, but they can also be established subtly or gradually over a large portion of the story. Another form of symbolism is **allusion**, which is when something in a story is used to prompt the reader to think about another work. Many well-known works use **Biblical allusions**, which are allusions to events or details in the Bible that inform a work or an element within it.

Language and Dialect

DIVERSITY AND SITUATIONAL NATURE OF LANGUAGE

Language is a diverse tool that allows people to communicate. However, language is often impacted and molded by the culture that uses it. This can make it difficult to learn and use a new language, since not all native speakers of the language will use it or interpret it the same way. For example, English is spoken all over America, but Americans in various regions of the country speak using different **dialects**. Other differences in speech include **accents** and **rhythm of speech**. Language is also manipulated by situations. Some terms and phrases have multiple meanings. A word's meaning often depends on the **context** in which the word or phrase is used, meaning that non-native speakers must learn to interpret situations to understand messages.

FACTORS OF LANGUAGE AND COMMUNICATION

INFLUENCES ON LANGUAGE

While dialect and diction are heavily influenced by an individual's culture and the location and history of the place they live, other personal factors can also impact language. A person's ethnicity, religious beliefs or background, and gender can influence the way they use and understand language. **Ethnicity** impacts language by incorporating a group's communication norms into an individual's speech and behavior. These norms may affect a speaker's tone, volume, or pace. These factors may lead others outside of that group to misinterpret the speaker's message, depending on their understanding of how those factors are used in speech. A person's **religious beliefs** can also affect their use of language. Religious beliefs and practices may lead an individual to abstain from using certain terms and may change the context in which a speaker uses specific words, or change their understanding of the word's usage. Additionally, a person may use language differently depending on their gender. **Gender's** influence on communication varies by region and industry. A region or industry's treatment of gender roles often impacts language use among its members. This can lead members of one gender group to be more assertive or submissive or to use different terms and phrases.

Culture and Communication

Individuals from different countries and cultures communicate differently. Not only do many people speak different languages, but they also speak using different inflections, volumes, tones, and dialects. These factors can have a significant impact on communication, even if the communicators speak the same language. In different cultures, certain behaviors are associated with different meanings and implications. When communicators from different cultures have a conversation, these expectations and associations may lead to misunderstanding. For example, Americans are considered to be louder and more demonstrative than people from other countries. Someone from a country where people speak more quietly who is not aware of this characterization may perceive an American's volume or large gestures as an indication of anger, when in reality, the American speaker is calm. The American may similarly perceive the other person as sad or shy due to their quiet voice, when the speaker is actually happy and comfortable in the conversation. Awareness of these factors and effects promotes respect for others and helps speakers understand the reasons for differences in communication, rather than allowing these differences to create division or conflict.

Language vs. Dialect

Languages are distinct and structured forms of verbal communication. Languages have cohesive sets of rules and words that are shared between the majority of that language's users. The main identifier of a language is that members of one language group are incapable of communicating fluently with members of another language group. New languages are formed as different dialects grow further apart until the members of each dialect can no longer innately communicate with each other.

Dialects are subsets of languages that do not violate the rules of the language as a whole, but which vary from other dialects in vocabulary usage, grammar forms, pronunciation, and spelling. Two major groupings of dialects are American and British English. Most American English and British English speakers can communicate with relative ease with one another, though the pronunciation, vocabulary (torch vs. flashlight; trunk vs. boot), spelling (meter vs. metre; color vs. colour), and grammar (in American English, collective nouns are always considered singular, but can be singular or plural in British English).

Development of Dialects over Time

Dialects are formed primarily through the influences of location and time, but can be the result of other elements of **social stratification** as well (economic, ethnic, religious, etc.). As one group of a language's speakers is separated from another, in British and American English speakers for example, the language develops in isolated locations at the same time, resulting in distinct dialects. Language changes continuously over time as new words and phrases are adopted and others are phased out. Eventually, these small changes result culminate into enough grammar and vocabulary changes that the speakers of the distinct dialects cannot easily communicate with one another. The dialects can then be recognized as distinct languages.

Use of Dialect in Media

Literary authors often use dialect when writing dialogue to illustrate the social and geographical backgrounds of specific characters, which supports character development. For example, in *The Adventures of Huckleberry Finn* (1885), Mark Twain's novel is written in the dialect of a young, uneducated, white, Southern character, opening with this sentence: "You don't know about me without you have read a book by the name of The Adventures of Tom Sawyer, but that ain't no matter." Twain uses a different and exaggerated dialect to represent the speech of the African-American slave Jim: "We's safe, Huck, we's safe! Jump up and crack yo' heels. Dat's de good ole Cairo at las', I jis knows it."

In *To Kill a Mockingbird,* author Harper Lee used dialect in the characters' dialogue to portray an uneducated boy in the American South: "Reckon I have. Almost died the first year I come to school and et them pecans—folks say he pizened 'em." Lee also uses many Southern regional expressions, such as "right stove up," "What in the sam holy hill?", "sit a spell," "fess" (meaning "confess"), "jim-dandy," and "hush your fussing." These contribute to Lee's characterization of the people she describes, who live in a small town in Alabama circa the 1930s. In *Wuthering Heights* (1847), Emily Bronte reproduces Britain's 18th–19th-century Yorkshire dialect in the speech of servant Joseph: "Running after t'lads, as usuald!... If I war yah, maister, I'd just slam t'boards i' their faces all on 'em, gentle and simple! Never a day ut yah're off, but yon cat o' Linton comes sneaking hither; and Miss Nelly, shoo's a fine lass!"

Dialect vs. Diction

When written as characters' dialogue in literary works, dialect represents the particular pronunciation, grammar, and figurative expressions used by certain groups of people based on their geographic region, social class, and cultural background. For example, when a character says, "There's gold up in them thar hills," the author is using dialect to add to the characterization of that individual. Diction is more related to individual characters than to groups of people. The way in which a specific character speaks, including his or her choice of words, manner of expressing himself or herself, and use of grammar all represent individual types of diction. For example, two characters in the same novel might describe the same action or event using different diction: One says "I'm heading uptown for the evening," and the other says "I'm going out for a night on the town." These convey the same literal meaning, but due to their variations in diction, the speakers are expressing themselves in slightly different ways.

Review Video: Dialogue, Paradox, and Dialect
Visit mometrix.com/academy and enter code: 684341

Influences on Regional Dialect

Linguistic researchers have identified regional variations in vocabulary choices, which have evolved because of differences in local climates and how they influence human behaviors. For example, in the Southern United States, the Linguistic Atlas of the Gulf States (LAGS) Project by Dr. Lee Pederson of Emory University discovered and documented that people living in the northern or Upland section of the Piedmont plateau region call the fungal infection commonly known as athlete's foot "toe itch," but people living in the southern or Lowland section call it "ground itch." The explanation for this difference is that in the north, temperatures are cooler and people wear shoes accordingly, so they associate the itching with the feet in their description, but in the south, temperatures are hotter and people often went barefoot, so they associated the itching with the ground that presumably transmitted the infection.

Using Dialect in Writing

Dialect is most appropriate for informal or creative writing. Using dialectal writing when communicating casually or informally, such as in a text message or a quick email to a peer, is acceptable. However, in academic and professional contexts, writing using indications of dialect is inappropriate and often unacceptable. If the audience includes individuals who have a higher rank than the author, or authority over the author, it is best not to write in a way that suggests a dialect.

World Literature

American Literary Periods

Dark Romantics

In American literature, a group of late Romantic writers are recognized as **Dark Romantics**. These authors' works may be associated with both the Romantic and Gothic movements. These works emphasize nature and emotion, aligning them with Romanticism, and include dark themes and tones, aligning them with Gothic literature. However, these works do not all feature the historically inspired characteristics of Gothic literature, and their morals or outcomes more closely resemble those of Romantic literature. The Dark Romantics include writers such as Edgar Allan Poe, Nathaniel Hawthorne, Emily Dickinson, and Herman Melville.

Transcendentalism

Transcendentalism was a smaller movement that occurred alongside the American Romantic movement. The **transcendentalists** shared the Romantic emphasis on emotion and also focused heavily on how a person experiences life through their senses. They extended these sentiments to suggest that through embracing one's senses, an individual could transcend, or experience a state of being above physical humanity. They also extended the Romantic emphasis on subjectivity through their praise of self-sufficiency, as exemplified through Ralph Waldo Emerson's *Self-Reliance*. Emerson was a prominent transcendentalist. His writings included an essay titled *Nature*, which explains a progression from the use of the senses to the achievement of transcendence. Transcendentalist literature includes several essays that discuss the value of the senses and emotions or the process of transcendence. Transcendentalists also wrote poetry that includes the frequent use of imagery, metaphors, and references to nature. These elements reflect the ideas of transcendentalism and create a resemblance to the alleged experience of transcendence. Ralph Waldo Emerson, Henry David Thoreau, and Walt Whitman were all prominent writers in this movement.

Colonial America

The **colonial era** in America was influenced by immigration from England to what is now New England. These immigrants were mainly Puritans who centered their society in New England on their religious beliefs, allowing those beliefs to inform all aspects of their lives. This is apparent in the literature of the time, as much of it includes essays and sermons that discuss religion or the way the Puritans believed one should live and conduct themselves. Colonial literature also includes many poems, and these works also discuss or reference religious ideas and themes. There was not much fiction written in Colonial America, as most of the literature was written to inform or persuade.

Romantic Period

The **American Romantic** movement is also known as the American Renaissance. This movement yielded several notable American writers and works that began characterizing American literature and differentiating it from British literature. This literature, written after the American Revolutionary War and until the end of the Civil War, praised individualism and featured an expression of national pride and patriotism. The transcendentalists' extreme ideas about self-sufficiency and subjectivity reiterated this individualism, and their recommendations about society and its structure furthered the separation of American literature from British literature. While this period shaped the definition of American literature, it is criticized for featuring a narrow view of

American politics and social issues at the time, as well as promoting a small group of similar writers.

Review Video: Authors in the Romantic Period
Visit mometrix.com/academy and enter code: 752719

Harlem Renaissance

The **Harlem Renaissance** took place in America during the 1920s and 1930s. The changing economy and opportunities led African Americans in the south to seek new lifestyles in other parts of America at the beginning of the 20th century. Many moved to Harlem, a small area in New York City. This group of African Americans yielded highly influential scholarly and artistic works, including poetry, fiction, music, and plays. The Harlem Renaissance marked an opportunity for these intellectuals and artists, who were largely ignored in the aftermath of the Civil War, to use their talents and express themselves through their works. While artists often featured personal expression in their works, the Harlem Renaissance was unique in its volume of culturally expressive works. This cultural expression and the movement's main ideas also contributed to the Civil Rights movement by promoting a spirit of unity among African Americans. The Harlem Renaissance eventually ended in the wake of the stock market crash in 1929. As the Great Depression began, financial support for the arts dwindled, making it difficult for many artists to succeed financially. Some members of the Harlem Renaissance who influenced American literature include Langston Hughes, Zora Neale Hurston, and Paul Robeson.

British Literary Periods

Neoclassical

The **British Neoclassical** period began in the middle of the 17th century and ended in the late 18th century. The latter part of the movement also took place alongside the Enlightenment, a period of scientific discovery and study that influenced many Western cultures. The Enlightenment's concern with intellectual pursuits and improvement increased discussions of introspection, or an individual's analysis of their own behavior, thoughts, and self. These ideas also affected society in England, as they contributed to a general attitude of complacency and a desire to ignore the past. The period saw a slightly increased acceptance of female writers, as their works were viewed as a method of self-reflection and improvement. The changes in British society allowed several new forms of literature to gain popularity and acceptance, usually for their introspective qualities. Essays, diaries, and letters all displayed the author's thoughts and experience, aligning them with the culture's values. Novels also gained popularity, as many were fictional diaries or epistolary novels. Journalism flourished during the Neoclassical period, leading to the creation of the newspaper. Literary criticism also gained popularity, though it was used to criticize an author and their style rather than examine or analyze the content of the work.

Victorian

The **Victorian Era** in England was influenced by a variety of events and ideas, many of which were influenced by the Victorians' economy. The Industrial Revolution in England changed the circumstances of work for the Victorians. The changing industries and lack of labor laws led to several problems and a wide division between Victorian social classes. These factors inspired and saturated much of Victorian literature. Many novels' plots and characters were heavily influenced by social and economic issues, and many poems referenced and criticized specific events that occurred during this period.

While the structure of Victorian society was a major influence on literature, there were other popular topics that appeared in literature. Topics like evolution, psychology, and colonization frequently appeared in Victorian literature, reflecting the concerns and interests of the Victorian culture. The Victorian society was also characterized by a strict moral code that supported the view of women as homemakers and criticized the idea of female writers. Not only did this affect the portrayal of women in literature, but it also led some female novelists, such as the Bronte sisters, to write under a pseudonym and present their works as having been written by a man. Victorian literature also popularized forms of literature, including the novel and the dramatic monologue, a poetic form developed by Robert Browning. Victorian writers include Charles Dickens, Oscar Wilde, Elizabeth Barrett Browning, Emily Bronte, Matthew Arnold, and Thomas Hardy.

World Literary Characteristics and Periods

While many other nations shared literary movements with America and England, there are numerous literary movements that are unique to other countries and cultures. Some of these literary movements can be understood as variations of movements like Romanticism or modernism, since they occurred at similar times and feature similar elements, but the political and cultural events of each country shaped their version of each movement. Most regions also have some type of mythology, and while different mythologies have similar characters and events, each region's mythology is unique and significant to the region's literature. Another common feature of world literature is colonialism. Many nations are former colonies of European countries, and the effects of colonization are present in modern literature from countries worldwide, making it a key feature of many regions' body of literature.

African Literature

Literature from some cultures was not recorded until the 19th century, causing any movements and trends to be informed by ideas told aloud. This is true of African literature, where stories and ideas were spoken and passed down through the generations. Early African poetry was often metaphorical, structured or written to form a paradox, and included a riddle or puzzling statement. Proverbs and didactic tales were also told frequently, reflecting the dominant religions in a given region and time period. These poems and stories also reflect the variety of languages spoken in Africa and the shifts in each language's usage. Early African literature, once people began writing it down, included stories and proverbs that had been passed down, translations of religious texts, and descriptions of the way of life in different African cultures or groups. These cultures and the events specific to each of them produce a unique body of literature that places emphasis on certain topics and ideas. For example, much of the modern literature written in South Africa discusses politics and issues of race, since the country's history is characterized by events and movements that revolved around these topics.

Asian Literature

Asian literature features writings from several different countries and languages and has spanned many centuries. Many popular forms of writing have come from Asia, such as the haiku. A couple of significant literary movements include The Hungry Generation in South Asia and the Misty Poets in China. The Hungry Generation is a literary movement involving literature written in the Bengali language, spoken mainly in West Bengal and Bangladesh. The literature is characterized by unique and innovative writing, which impacted the use of figurative language in the region. The Hungry Generation also discussed cultural issues, particularly colonization in the region, and many participants were arrested for their work. The Misty Poets in China were characterized by their expressive use of abstractions. Their name, Misty Poets, comes from their writings, which were difficult to interpret due to their use of abstract language and ambiguity. This movement was partly inspired by the Misty Poets' distaste for literary realism, though its influence is detectable within their poetry. Many of the Misty Poets were punished for their poetry, since the poetry of this movement was also politically critical.

Latin American Literature

Latin American literature has several literary movements, many of which occurred near the same time as American and British literary movements and share ideas and trends with their English counterparts. Despite these similarities, each of these movements is distinguishable as its own movement with unique impacts of Latin American literature. By the 17th century, written language was in use in Mexico, and Latin American literary trends and figures had been recognized. During the 18th century, Latin American literature featured a variety of ideas and themes within each form of literature. By the 19th century, literary themes were more unified throughout popular Latin American literature. In the early 19th century, Latin American literature embraced the Romantic movement as it came to an end in England and the United States. Several Latin American countries were also fighting for independence during this time, amplifying the Romantic idea of national pride and identity.

In the wake of the Romantic movement, Latin American literature introduced the unique *Modernismo* movement, which yielded a large volume of poetry and is characterized by the use of whimsical imagery and discussions of spiritual ideas. Following *Modernismo* was the *Vanguardia* movement, which was created to introduce diversity within Latin American literature after modernism permeated the literature of the time. *Vanguardia* involved writers taking risks in their writing and breaking the mold from typical Latin American literature. In the 20th century, *Estridentismo* followed the *Vanguardia* movement, marrying the *Vanguardia* movement with the European Avant-Garde movement. Other 20th century movements functioned similarly by adapting literary movements from other regions to suit the themes and trends in Latin American literature, reflect Latin American cultures, and set their literature apart from other cultures.

Literary Periods and Movements

Old English

The English language developed over a long period of time through interactions between different groups in Europe, including the Romans, the Germans, and the Celtics. The Anglo-Saxons, a group that left what is now Germany and settled in England, further established the English language by using what is now called **Old English**. While Old English laid foundations for modern English, its usage fundamentally differs from the way English is used today. For example, Old English relied on inflections to create meaning, placing little importance on the order of the words in the sentence. Its use of verbs and tenses also differs from modern English grammar. The Anglo-Saxons also used kennings, or compound words that functioned as figurative language.

Old English, as a language influenced by several cultures, had dialects from its inception. Differences in usage also came from the division between secular and religious cultures. This division heavily influenced Old English literature, as most of the literature from the time is categorized according to the set of beliefs it reflects. Most of the influential literature of the time includes riddles, poems, or translations of religious texts. Surviving Old English poetry mainly discusses real heroes and battles or provides a narrative about a fictional hero. Many of these fictional poems are considered *lays*, or *lais*, which are narrative poems that are structured using couplets of lines containing eight syllables each. The translations were often of passages from the Christian Bible, adaptations of Biblical passages, or copies of Christian hymns. Old English persisted until the 12th century, where it was eventually replaced with Middle English. Influential literature from this period includes *Beowulf*, "The Wanderer," "The Wife's Lament," and "The Seafarer."

MIDDLE ENGLISH

Old English was replaced by **Middle English**, which was used from the 12th century to the 16th century. Old English was not governed by a consistent set of grammatical rules until the Norse people, their language, and its structure influenced the integration of grammar into English, leading to Middle English. Middle English relied less on inflections than Old English, instead creating variations by using affixes and synonyms. The development of grammar was further facilitated by the printing press, which made it easier for writers to comply with grammar rules since the printing of identical copies reduced variation between texts.

Old English's evolution into Middle English can be narrowed down to three stages: Early, Central, and Late Middle English. Early Middle English, though it showed a change in the language, maintained the writing style of Old English. Central Middle English is characterized by the development of dialects within written communication, which is partly due to scribes who translated texts or parts of texts using terms from their own dialect, rather than the source. Late Middle English includes numerous developments that created the foundation for Modern English. *The Canterbury Tales*, "Sir Gawain and the Green Knight," and "Le Morte d'Arthur" are all Middle English texts that are still read and studied today.

THE RENAISSANCE

The **Renaissance** swept through Europe and lasted for multiple centuries, bringing many developments in culture, the arts, education, and philosophy. The Renaissance in England did not begin until the late 15th century. Though ideas and cultures of the past, especially those of the ancient Greeks and Romans, inspired the Renaissance, the period saw innumerable developments in the English language and literature. The Renaissance was characterized by a focus on the humanities, allowing the arts, including literature, to flourish. At the time, drama was possibly the most popular form of literature, as the popularity of plays and theatrical performances greatly increased. Much of Renaissance literature is still studied today, maintaining its influence on Western literature. Poetry was also popular, and the period saw the development of new forms of poetry, such as the sonnet. Sonnets are often recognized according to one of four styles, each of which was popularized by a Renaissance writer. Lyrical poetry, which discusses emotions and is often written using first-person point of view, was also popular during the Renaissance.

In addition to new forms and literary trends, the Renaissance period also impacted English literature by facilitating discussion over the translation of the Bible. Education at the time often included instruction in Greek and Latin, allowing those with an education to read ancient texts in their original language. However, this instruction did not reach the majority of the public. The Protestant Reformation encouraged discussions about translating the Bible to make it accessible to more people. This suggestion was challenged by those who doubted the ability of the English language to fully reflect the original text. Eventually, the Bible was translated to English, and William Tyndale's partial translation became especially influential for later translations and the continuing development of the English language. Influential writers of the English Renaissance include William Shakespeare, John Donne, John Milton, Edmund Spenser, and Christopher Marlowe.

GOTHIC

The Gothic literary movement, beginning in the 18th century and persisting through the 19th century, took inspiration from the architecture and cultures of the Late Middle Ages in Europe. The Late Middle Ages saw the popularity of Gothic architecture, most prominently in places of worship. These structures inspired many of the settings in **Gothic literature**, as a large volume of Gothic literature takes place in an impressive location, such as a castle or ornate mansion. Gothic works also are often set in the past, long before the time the story was written. This aligns with prominent themes in Gothic literature, as several pieces are informed by an event that occurred before the story begins or a character who died before the plot's first event.

Another common characteristic of Gothic literature is its eerie, dark, suspenseful tone. Authors of Gothic literature often created this tone by setting their works in secluded and strange locations and incorporating intense, unsettling, or even supernatural events and scenarios into the plot. This tone is also created through the theme of death or mortality that often appears in Gothic literature. These characteristics support the aim of many Gothic writers to create fiction that evokes a certain emotion from the reader or shapes their reading experience. Well-known authors of Gothic literature include Horace Walpole, Ann Radcliffe, Edgar Allan Poe, and Nathaniel Hawthorne. While the Gothic literary movement took place in the 18th and 19th centuries, many works have been published in more recent centuries that have several characteristics of Gothic literature and may be included within the overall Gothic genre.

NATURALISM

Naturalism was an active literary movement in the late 19th century, taking place alongside movements such as realism and modernism. **Naturalism**, like realism, rejected the emotional focus and sentimentality of Romanticism and provided a type of social commentary. However, the naturalist movement stretched the ideas of realism, promoting literature that authentically depicts the life of the common man and criticizing the influence of morality on such literature. Naturalist literature often includes characters who belong to a lower class and experience circumstances beyond their own control and takes place in urban settings. Prominent themes in naturalist literature include nature as an apathetic force, the influence of heredity, and life as something to be endured and survived. One of the most influential naturalist writers is French writer Emile Zola. Influential American Naturalists include Stephen Crane, Hamlin Garland, and Theodore Dreiser.

MODERNISM

The Modernist literary movement was largely influenced by industrialization, which heavily impacted both the Unites States and England, primarily in the 19th century. **Modernism** in literature was characterized by an attempt to turn away from the norms and traditions of literature and use new techniques and methods. Modernist literature was often written in first person and used literary devices and techniques to reveal problems within society. For the American modernists, these societal changes came from industrialization and the first World War, which effected the general view of human nature and reliability. In England, there were additional factors contributing to this shift. Modernism began during Queen Victoria's reign, which defined the period known as the Victorian Era. The Victorian society was characterized by a strict moral code that permeated England's society at the time. This moral code was incompatible with the Modernist's desire to turn away from tradition, but the changes that accompanied Victoria's death in 1901 enabled the Modernist movement to grow in England. American Modernist writers include Ezra Pound, William Carlos Williams, and Gertrude Stein. British Modernist writers include Matthew Arnold, William Butler Yeats, T. S. Eliot, and Joseph Conrad.

POSTMODERNISM

Postmodernism grew out of Modernism's reliance on science and universal assertions, but emphasized the individual's subjective perception of reality, as it is often more authentic to an individual's experience than a universally applied statement. Postmodernism asserts that since each person creates their own version of reality, fully and accurately defining reality is futile and impossible. Due to this skepticism, postmodern writers use many concrete details, rather than abstract details, because they can be objectively observed and are not left up to the individual. The postmodernist literary movement began around the 1960s. The literary movement included a variety of new genres and techniques, reflecting the postmodernist idea that things like art cannot be truly defined or simplified. Notable American writers of the postmodernist movement include Kurt Vonnegut, John Barth, and Thomas Pynchon. British postmodernist writers include John Fowles and Julian Barnes.

Public Speaking

Speeches

Speeches are written to be delivered in spoken language in public, to various groups of people, at formal or informal events. Some generic types include welcome speeches, thank-you speeches, keynote addresses, position papers, commemorative and dedication speeches, and farewell speeches. Speeches are commonly written in present tense and usually begin with an introduction greeting the audience. At official functions, specific audience members are named ("Chairperson [name]," "Principal [name], teachers, and students," etc.) and when audiences include a distinguished guest, he or she is often named as well. Then the speaker introduces him or herself by name, position, and department or organization as applicable. After the greeting, the speaker then introduces the topic and states the purpose of the speech. The body of the speech follows, similarly to the body of an essay, stating its main points, an explanation of each point, and supporting evidence. Finally, in the conclusion, the speaker states his or her hope for accomplishing the speech's purpose and thanks the audience for attending and listening to the speech.

Clearly Written Prose and Speeches

To achieve **clarity**, a writer or speaker must first define his or her purpose carefully. The speech should be organized logically, so that sentences make sense and follow each other in an understandable order. Sentences must also be constructed well, with carefully chosen words and structure. Organizing a speech in advance using an outline provides the writer or speaker with a blueprint, directing and focusing the composition to meet its intended purpose. Organized speeches enable audiences to comprehend and retain the presented information more easily. Humans naturally seek to impose order on the world by seeking patterns. Hence, when ideas in a speech are well-organized and adhere to a consistent pattern, the speaker communicates better with listeners and is more convincing. Speechwriters can use chronological patterns to organize events, sequential patterns to organize processes by their steps, and spatial patterns to help audiences visualize geographical locations and movements or physical scenarios. Also, comparison-contrast patterns give audiences insight about similarities and differences between and among topics, especially when listeners are more familiar with one than the other.

Evaluating Speeches for Concise Information

To convince or persuade listeners or reinforce a message, speeches must be succinct. Audiences can become confused by excessive anecdotes and details. If a speaker takes three minutes or more to get to the point, audience members' attention will start to fade and will only worsen when details deviate from the main subject. When answering a question, the asker and speaker may even forget the original question if the speaker takes too long. Speakers should practice not only rehearsing written speeches, but also developing skill for spontaneous question-and-answer sessions after speeches. Speakers should differentiate necessary from simply interesting information because audiences can become overwhelmed by too much information. Speakers should know what points they wish to make. They should not be afraid to pause before responding to questions, which indicates thoughtfulness and control rather than lack of knowledge. Restating questions increases comprehension and appropriate responses, and allows time to form answers mentally.

Organizational Patterns for Speeches

A speechwriter who uses an **advantages-disadvantages** pattern of organization presents the audience with the pros and cons of a topic. This aids writers in discussing two sides of an issue objectively without an argumentative position, enabling listeners to weigh both aspects. When a speechwriter uses a **cause-and-effect** pattern, it can help to persuade audiences to agree with an action or solution by showing significant relationships between factors. Writers may separate an outline into two main "cause" and "effect" sections or into separate sections for each cause, including the effect for each. Persuasive writing also benefits from **problem-solution** patterns: by establishing the existence of a problem, writers induce audiences to realize a need for change. By supplying a solution and supporting its superiority above other solutions, the writer convinces audiences of the value of that solution. When none of these patterns—or **chronological**, **sequential**, **spatial**, or **comparison-contrast** patterns—applies, speechwriters often use topical patterns. These organize information by various subtopics and types within the main topic or category.

Effective Speech Delivery

Speakers should deliver speeches in a natural, conversational manner rather than being rigidly formal or theatrical. Effective delivery is also supported by confidence. Speakers should be direct, building audience rapport through personal connection and vivid imagery. Speakers should be mindful of the occasion, subject, and audience of their speeches and take care to use appropriate language. Good speakers learn vocal control, including volume, speed, pitch, use of pauses, tonal variety, correct pronunciation, and clear articulation. They can express enthusiasm and emphasize important points with their voices. Nonverbal behaviors, such as eye contact, facial expressions, gestures, good posture, and body movements clarify communication, stress important ideas, and influence perceptions that the speaker is trustworthy, competent, and credible. Nonverbal communications should seem as spontaneous and natural as vocal or verbal ones. Speakers should know their speeches well and practice frequently, taking care to avoid nervous or irrelevant movements such as tapping or pacing.

Media Types

Media and Format Choices

Effective communication depends on choosing the correct method. Media and format choices are influenced by the target audience, the budget, and the needs of the audience.

Instructional Videos

Instructional videos have potential for excellent two-way communication because questions and feedback can be built in. Videos can be targeted to particular audiences, and they can be paused for discussion or replayed to reinforce concepts. Viewers can see processes, including "before," "during," and "after" phases. Videos are accessible because most communities have at least one DVD player or computer. Moreover, video players and computers are continually becoming less expensive to buy and use. Disadvantages include the necessity of editing software and equipment in some cases, as well as the need for support from other print materials. There is also danger of overuse, if other media or methods are more appropriate, and higher up-front costs. Producers of instructional videos must account for the costs of script development and hiring local performers as needed.

DVDs and CDs

Interactive DVDs and CDs, such as games, give viewers the opportunity to actively participate as they learn information. Additionally, videos are considered to be a professional method of sharing information. Compared to many other media formats, discs are comparatively inexpensive to make and are easy to transport due to their small size and weight. They are more resistant to damage and aging than older videotape technology, making them more durable. Some disadvantages include needing access to technology to play what is stored on the disc and access to certain software programs to add new content to a disc, especially if the producer wants to include video animation or audio commentary. Producers must also consider expenses concerning paid staff and production and labeling expenses. Content that would appear on DVDs and CDs can alternatively be shared through streaming services or digital files stored on a computer or other compatible device.

Television and Radio

Both television and radio are forms of mass media that reach many people. TV has the broadest reach and can market to the general public or be customized for target audiences, while radio only tends to reach specific target audiences. TV has the advantage of video plus audio, while radio broadcasts only feature audio. However, access to television programs is more expensive than access to radio broadcasts. A shared disadvantage is that TV and radio audiences can only interact directly during call-in programs. Additionally, programming times may be inconvenient, but tape, digital sound, and digital video recording (DVR) can remedy this. Many streaming services also provide access to these programs. Both television and radio are useful for communicating simple slogans and messages, and both can generate awareness, interest, and excitement.

Newspapers

Except for the occasional community columns, news releases, and letters to the editor, newspaper pages and features afford little opportunity for audience input or participation. However, they do reach and appeal to the general public. Cost is an advantage: hiring a PR writer and paying for a news advertisement costs much less than a radio or TV spot. Additionally, newspaper features are high-status, and audiences can reread and review them as often as they like. However, newspaper ads may have difficulty affecting the reader as deeply without audio or video, and they require a literate audience. Their publication is also subject to editors' whims and biases. Newspaper pieces combining advertising and editorial content—"advertorials"—provide inclusion of paid material, but are viewed as medium-status and cost more.

Websites, Blogs, Mobile Phones, and Text Messaging

Computer literacy is required for online material, but participation potential is high via websites, e-networking, and blogging. Mobile phones and text messaging are used for enormous direct, public, two-way and one-on-one communication, with timely information and reminders. Web media need a literate public and can be tailored for specific audiences. They afford global information, are accessible by increasingly technology-literate populations, and are high-status. Web media disadvantages include the necessity of computers and people to design, manage, and supply content, as well as to provide technical support. Mobile and text media are globally popular, but appeal especially to certain demographics like teens and young adults. They are increasingly available, especially in rural regions, and are decreasing in cost. Mobile and text media disadvantages include required brevity in texts and provider messaging charges. Links to related websites and pages within existing sites are also advantages of digital media.

Public Presentations and Slideshows

Public presentations have great potential for audience participation and can directly target various audiences. They can encourage the establishment of partnerships and groups, stimulate local ownership of issues and projects, and make information public. A drawback to public presentations is that they are limited to nights, weekends, or whenever audiences are available and do not always attract the intended audience.

Another method of presentation is to use **slideshows**. These presentations are best for sophisticated audiences like professionals, civil servants, and service organizations. Well-designed slideshows are good for stimulating audience interest, selling ideas, and marketing products. Also, they are accessible online as well as in-person so they can reach a broader audience. Slideshow disadvantages include the necessity of projectors and other equipment. They are also limited to communicating more general points, outlines, and summaries rather than conveying a multitude of information in more detail.

Posters and Brochures

Both **posters** and **brochures** can target audiences of the general public and more specific public sectors. Posters are better for communicating simple slogans and messages, while brochures can include more detail and are better for printing instructional information. Both can be inexpensive to produce, especially if printed only as needed and in-house. Posters can often be printed in-house without using outside printing companies. However, it is difficult to get feedback on both posters and brochures—unless they have been broadly tested, or if their publication is accompanied by workshops and other participatory events. A disadvantage of using posters is that they are designed to draw attention and communicate quickly, as they are mostly viewed in passing. This means that their messages must be simple and communicate efficiently. A disadvantage of using brochures is that they can only be distributed to a specific, limited group or area. Posters and brochures are also only understood when audiences are literate in both written language and visual elements.

Flyers and Fact Sheets

Flyers and fact sheets have one-way communication potential because readers cannot give feedback. Their target audiences are general. Some advantages of using this form of media include flexibility: people can distribute them at meetings or events, put them on car windshields in parking lots, leave them in stores or on bulletin boards at community agencies and schools, hand them out from booths and other displays, or mail them. When printed in black and white, they can be very inexpensive. They afford recipients the convenience of being able to review them at their leisure. Organizations and individuals can produce flyers and fact sheets in-house, or even at home with desktop publishing software. Disadvantages include their limitation to single facts or tips and specific information on specified topics.

Evaluating Media Information Sources

With the wealth of media in different formats available today, users are more likely to take media at face value. However, to understand the content of media, consumers must **critically evaluate each source**.

Users should ask themselves the following questions about media sources:

- Who is delivering this message and why?
- What methods do a media source's publishers employ to gain and maintain users' attention?
- Which points of view is the media source representing?
- What are the various ways this message could be interpreted?
- What information is missing from the message?
- Is the source scholarly, i.e., peer-reviewed?

- Does it include author names and their credentials as they relate to the topic?
- Who publishes it and why?
- Who is the target audience?
- Is the language technically specific or non-technical?
- Are sources cited, research claims documented, conclusions based on furnished evidence, and references provided?
- Is the publication current?

Other Considerations for the Validity of Sources

For books, consider whether information is **up-to-date** and whether **historical perspectives** apply. Content is more likely to be **scholarly** if publishers are universities, government, or professional organizations. Book reviews can also provide useful information. For articles, identify the author, publisher, frequency of the periodical's publication, and what kind of advertising, if any, is included. Looking for book reviews also informs users. For articles, look for biographical author information, publisher name, frequency of the periodical's publication, and whether advertising is included and, if so, whether it is for certain occupations or disciplines. For web pages, check their domain names, identify publishers or sponsors, look for the author or publisher's contact information, check dates of most recent page updates, be alert to biases, and verify the validity of the information on the webpage. The quality and accuracy of web pages located through search engines rather than library databases varies widely and requires careful user inspection. Web page recommendations from reliable sources like university faculties can help indicate quality and accuracy. Citations of websites by credible or scholarly sources also show reliability. Authors' names, relevant credentials, affiliations, and contact information support their authority. Site functionality, such as ease of navigation, ability to search, site maps, and indexes, is also a criterion to consider.

Persuasive Media

Advertising, public relations, and advocacy media all use **persuasion**. Advertisers use persuasion to sell goods and services. The public relations field uses persuasion to give good impressions of companies, governments, or organizations. Advocacy groups use persuasion to garner support or votes. Persuasion can come through commercials, public service announcements, speeches, websites, and newsletters, among other channels. Activists, lobbyists, government officials, and politicians use political rhetoric involving persuasive techniques. Basic techniques include using celebrity spokespersons, whom consumers admire or aspire to resemble, or conversely, "everyday people" (albeit often portrayed by actors) with whom consumers identify. Using expert testimonials lends credibility. Explicit claims of content, effectiveness, quality, and reliability—which often cannot be proven or disproven—are used to persuade. While news and advocacy messages mostly eschew humor for credibility's sake (except in political satire), advertising often persuades via humor, which gets consumer attention and associates its pleasure with advertised products and services. Qualifiers and other misleading terms, sometimes called "Weasel words," are often combined with exaggerated claims. Intensifiers, such as hyperboles, superlatives, repetitions, and sentimental appeals are also persuasive.

Intermediate Techniques

Dangerous propagandist Adolf Hitler said people suspect little lies more than big ones; hence the "Big Lie" is a persuasion method that cannot be identified without consumers' keen critical thinking. A related method is **charisma**, which can induce people to believe messages they would otherwise reject. **Euphemisms** substitute abstract, vague, or bland terms in place of more graphic, clear, and unpleasant ones. For example, the terms "layoffs" and "firing" are replaced by "downsizing," and "torture" is replaced with "intensive interrogation techniques." **Extrapolation** bases sweeping conclusions on small amounts of minor information to appeal to what consumers wish or hope. Flattery appeals to consumer self-esteem needs, such as L'Oréal's "You're worth it." Flattery is sometimes accomplished through contrast, like ads showing others' mistakes to make consumers feel superior and smarter. "Glittering generalities" refer to claims based on concepts such as beauty, love, health, democracy, freedom, and science. Persuaders use this tactic to gain consumer acceptance without consumers questioning what they mean. The opposite is name-calling to persuade consumers to reject someone or something.

American citizens love new ideas and technology. Persuaders exploit this by emphasizing the **newness** of products, services, and candidates. Conversely, they also use **nostalgia** to evoke consumers' happy memories, which they often remember more than unhappy ones. Citing "scientific evidence" is an intermediate version of the basic technique of expert testimonials. Consumers may accept this as proof, but some advertisers, politicians, and other persuaders may present inaccurate or misleading "evidence." Another intermediate technique is the "simple solution." Although the natures of people and life are complex, when consumers feel overwhelmed by complexity, persuaders exploit this by offering policies, products, or services they claim will solve complicated problems by simple means. Persuaders also use symbols, images, words, and names we associate with more general, emotional concepts like lifestyle, country, family, religion, and gender. While symbols have power, their significance also varies across individuals. For example, some consumers regard the Hummer SUV as a prestigious status symbol, while others regard it as environmentally harmful and irresponsible.

ADVANCED TECHNIQUES

Ad hominem, Latin for "against the man" attacks the person behind an idea rather than criticizing the idea itself. It operates by association: if a person is considered immoral or uneducated, then his or her ideas must be bad as well. **"Stacking the deck"** misleads by presenting only selected information that supports one position. **Apophasis**, or a false denial, allows the speaker or writer to indirectly bring attention to a flaw in an opponent's credibility. For example, a politician saying, "I won't mention my opponent's tax evasion issues" manages to mention them while seeming less accusatory. Persuaders may also use **majority belief**, making statements such as "Four out of five dentists recommend this brand" or "[insert number] people can't be wrong." In an intensified version, persuaders exploit group dynamics at rallies, speeches, and other live-audience events where people are vulnerable to surrounding crowd influences. **Scapegoating**, blaming one person or group for complex problems, is a form of the intermediate "simple solution" technique, a practice common in politics. **Timing** also persuades, like advertising flowers and candy in the weeks preceding Valentine's Day, ad campaigns preceding new technology rollouts, and politician speeches following big news events.

VISUAL MEDIA

Some images have the power to communicate more information than an entire paragraph. Images can contain several elements and be interpreted different ways, making them an effective vessel for abstract and emotionally appealing ideas. Humans are also able to understand images before they fully acquire language, meaning that images can reach more people than language can at any time. Images are also more quickly comprehended than text, making them a highly efficient method of communication. People can remember or memorize images more easily than text, also. Historically, images have been used for propaganda and subliminal messaging. Images are also used by different companies as an effective technique to entice customers to buy their products. Though images do not always contain text, they can still convey explicit and implicit meanings. An image's explicit meaning would be the most recognizable shape or concept in the image. The implicit meaning may be obscured within the image through the use of negative space, background images, or out-of-focus shapes.

Interpreting and Evaluating Persuasive Media

Most messages can be interpreted in different ways. They can be interpreted explicitly, where the literal meaning of the words in the message creates the meaning of the message, and no context is considered. Alternatively, other contexts can be considered alongside the explicit meaning of the message. These create alternative, not clearly stated meanings called **implicit meanings**. Politics, current events, regional norms, and even emotions are examples of contexts that can add implicit meanings to a message. These implicit meanings can change the effect a message has on its recipient. Many products have slogans with both implicit and explicit meanings. These implicit meanings must be considered to fully interpret a message.

Messages come in different forms, and each form has a unique way of communicating both explicit and implicit meanings. Images can come with captions that communicate a message, but some images carry subliminal messages. This means that their implicit meaning is received by the viewer, but the viewer is not aware of it. The term **propaganda** describes messages that advocate for a specific opinion or way of thinking. Most propaganda is politically driven and has been used during historical periods, most notably World War II. Unlike messages with hidden or veiled implicit meanings, most propaganda aggressively communicates its entire meaning and is difficult to misinterpret. Documentaries are another prominent form of communication. Documentaries are informational videos that focus on a specific figure, subject, phenomenon, or time period. While documentaries are primarily fact based and contain excerpts from interviews and testimonials, documentaries feature a limited view of their subject and sometimes attempt to persuade viewers to take action or embrace their central message. While some documentaries communicate this clearly, some hide an implicit meaning through the way they present each piece of information.

Developmental Literacy

Literacy

Literacy is commonly understood as the **ability to read and write**. UNESCO, the United Nations Educational, Scientific, and Cultural Organization, has further defined literacy as the "ability to identify, understand, interpret, create, communicate, compute, and use printed and written materials associated with varying contexts." Under the UNESCO definition, understanding cultural, political, and historical contexts of communities falls under the definition of literacy. While **reading literacy** may be gauged simply by the ability to read a newspaper, **writing literacy** includes spelling, grammar, and sentence structure. To be literate in a foreign language, one would also need to be able to understand a language by listening and be able to speak the language. Some argue that visual representation and numeracy should be included in the requirements one must meet to be considered literate. **Computer literacy** refers to one's ability to utilize the basic functions of computers and other technologies. Subsets of reading literacy include phonological awareness, decoding, comprehension, and vocabulary.

Phonological Awareness

A subskill of literacy, phonological awareness is the ability to perceive sound structures in a spoken word, such as syllables and the individual phonemes within syllables. **Phonemes** are the sounds represented by the letters in the alphabet. The ability to separate, blend, and manipulate sounds is critical to developing reading and spelling skills. Phonological awareness is concerned with not only syllables, but also **onset sounds** (the initial sound in a word, such as /k/ in 'cat') and **rime** (the sounds that follow the onset in a word, such as /at/ in 'cat'). Phonological awareness is an auditory skill that does not necessarily involve print. It should be developed before the student has learned letter to sound correspondences. A student's phonological awareness is an indicator of future reading success.

> **Review Video: Phonological and Phonemic Awareness, and Phonics**
> Visit mometrix.com/academy and enter code: 197017
>
> **Review Video: Components of Oral Language Development**
> Visit mometrix.com/academy and enter code: 480589

Communication Development Normally Occurring Within a Child's First Five Years of Life

Language and communication development depend strongly on the language a child develops within the first five years of life. During this time, three developmental periods are observed. At birth, the first period begins. This period is characterized by infant crying and gazing. Babies communicate their sensations and emotions through these behaviors, so they are expressive; however, they are not yet intentional. They indirectly indicate their needs through expressing how they feel, and when these needs are met, these communicative behaviors are reinforced. These expressions and reinforcement are the foundations for the later development of intentional communication. This becomes possible in the second developmental period, between 6 and 18 months. At this time, infants become able to coordinate their attention visually with other people relative to things and events, enabling purposeful communication with adults. During the third developmental period, from 18 months on, children come to use language as their main way of communicating and learning. Preschoolers can carry on conversations, exercise self-control through language use, and conduct verbal negotiations.

Milestones of Normal Language Development by the 2 Years Old

By the time most children reach the age of 2 years, they have acquired a vocabulary of about 150 to 300 words. They can name various familiar objects found in their environments. They are able to use at least two prepositions in their speech (e.g., *in*, *on*, and/or *under*). Two-year-olds typically combine the words they know into short sentences. These sentences tend to be mostly noun-verb or verb-noun combinations (e.g., "Daddy work," "Watch this"). They may also include verb-preposition combinations (e.g., "Go out," "Come in"). By the age of 2 years, children use pronouns, such as *I*, *me*, and *you*. They typically can use at least two such pronouns correctly. A normally developing 2-year-old will respond to some commands, directions, or questions, such as "Show me your eyes" or "Where are your ears?"

Salient General Aspects of Human Language Abilities from Before Birth to 5 Years of Age

Language and communication abilities are integral parts of human life that are central to learning, successful school performance, successful social interactions, and successful living. Human language ability begins before birth: the developing fetus can hear not only internal maternal sounds, but also the mother's voice, others' voices, and other sounds outside the womb. Humans have a natural sensitivity to human sounds and languages from before they are born until they are about 4½ years old. These years are critical for developing language and communication. Babies and young children are predisposed to greater sensitivity to human sounds than other sounds, orienting them toward the language spoken around them. Children absorb their environmental language completely, including vocal tones, syntax, usage, and emphasis. This linguistic absorption occurs very rapidly. Children's first 2½ years particularly involve amazing abilities to learn language, including grammatical expression.

6 Months, 12 Months, and 18 Months

Individual differences dictate a broad range of language development that is still normal. However, parents observing noticeably delayed language development in their children should consult professionals. Typically, babies respond to hearing their names by 6 months of age, turn their heads and eyes toward the sources of human voices they hear, and respond accordingly to friendly and angry tones of voice. By the age of 12 months, toddlers can usually understand and follow simple directions, especially when these are accompanied by physical and/or vocal cues. They can intentionally use one or more words with the correct meaning. By the age of 18 months, a normally developing child usually has acquired a vocabulary of roughly 5 to 20 words. Eighteen-month-old children use nouns in their speech most of the time. They are very likely to repeat certain words and/or phrases over and over. At this age, children typically are able to follow simple verbal commands without needing as many visual or auditory cues as at 12 months.

Three Years

By the time they are 3 years old, most normally developing children have acquired vocabularies of between 900 and 1,000 words. Typically, they correctly use the pronouns *I*, *me*, and *you*. They use more verbs more frequently. They apply past tenses to some verbs and plurals to some nouns. 3-year-olds usually can use at least three prepositions; the most common are *in*, *on*, and *under*. The normally developing 3-year-old knows the major body parts and can name them. 3-year-olds typically use 3-word sentences with ease. Normally, parents should find approximately 75 to 100 percent of what a 3-year-old says to be intelligible, while strangers should find between 50 and 75 percent of a 3-year-old's speech intelligible. Children this age comprehend most simple questions about their activities and environments and can answer questions about what they should do when they are thirsty, hungry, sleepy, hot, or cold. They can tell about their experiences in ways that adults can generally follow. By the age of 3 years, children should also be able to tell others their name, age, and sex.

Four Years

When normally developing children are 4 years old, most know the names of animals familiar to them. They can use at least four prepositions in their speech (e.g., *in*, *on*, *under*, *to*, *from*, etc.). They can name familiar objects in pictures, and they know and can identify one color or more. Usually, they are able to repeat four-syllable words they hear. They verbalize as they engage in their activities, which Vygotsky dubbed "private speech." Private speech helps young children think through what they are doing, solve problems, make decisions, and reinforce the correct sequences in multistep activities. When presented with contrasting items, 4-year-olds can understand comparative concepts like bigger and smaller. At this age, they are able to comply with simple commands without the target stimuli being in their sight (e.g., "Put those clothes in the hamper" [upstairs]). Four-year-old children will also frequently repeat speech sounds, syllables, words, and phrases, similar to 18-month-olds' repetitions but at higher linguistic and developmental levels.

Five Years

Once most children have reached the age of 5 years, their speech has expanded from the emphasis of younger children on nouns, verbs, and a few prepositions, and is now characterized by many more descriptive words, including adjectives and adverbs. Five-year-olds understand common antonyms, such as big/little, heavy/light, long/short, and hot/cold. They can now repeat longer sentences they hear, up to about 9 words. When given three consecutive, uninterrupted commands, the typical 5-year-old can follow these without forgetting one or two. At age 5, most children have learned simple concepts of time like today, yesterday, and tomorrow; day, morning, afternoon, and night; and before, after, and later. Five-year-olds typically speak in relatively long sentences and normally should be incorporating some compound sentences (with more than one independent clause) and complex sentences (with one or more independent and dependent clauses). Five-year-old children's speech is also grammatically correct most of the time.

Activities That Teach Phonological Awareness

Classroom activities that teach phonological awareness include language play and exposure to a variety of sounds and the contexts of sounds. Activities that teach phonological awareness include:

- Clapping to the sounds of individual words, names, or all words in a sentence
- Practicing saying blended phonemes
- Singing songs that involve phoneme replacement (e.g., The Name Game)
- Reading poems, songs, and nursery rhymes out loud
- Reading patterned and predictable texts out loud
- Listening to environmental sounds or following verbal directions
- Playing games with rhyming chants or fingerplays
- Reading alliterative texts out loud
- Grouping objects by beginning sounds
- Reordering words in a well-known sentence or making silly phrases by deleting words from a well-known sentence (perhaps from a favorite storybook)

Teaching of Reading Through Phonics

Phonics is the process of learning to read by learning how spoken language is represented by letters. Students learn to read phonetically by sounding out the **phonemes** in words and then blending them together to produce the correct sounds in words. In other words, the student connects speech sounds with letters or groups of letters and blends the sounds together to determine the pronunciation of an unknown word. Phonics is a method commonly used to teach **decoding and reading**, but it has been challenged by other methods, such as the whole language approach. Despite the complexity of pronunciation and combined sounds in the English language, phonics is a highly effective way to teach reading. Being able to read or pronounce a word does not mean the student comprehends the meaning of the word, but context aids comprehension. When phonics is used as a foundation for decoding, children eventually learn to recognize words automatically and advance to decoding multisyllable words with practice.

Alphabetic Principle and Alphabet Writing Systems

The **alphabetic principle** refers to the use of letters and combinations of letters to represent speech sounds. The way letters are combined and pronounced is guided by a system of rules that establishes relationships between written and spoken words and their letter symbols. Alphabet writing systems are common around the world. Some are **phonological** in that each letter stands for an individual sound and words are spelled just as they sound. However, keep in mind that there are other writing systems as well, such as the Chinese **logographic** system and the Japanese **syllabic** system.

Review Video: Print Awareness and Alphabet Knowledge
Visit mometrix.com/academy and enter code: 541069

Facts Children Should Know About Letters

To be appropriately prepared to learn to read and write, a child should learn:

- That each letter is **distinct** in appearance
- What **direction and shape** must be used to write each letter
- That each letter has a **name**, which can be associated with the shape of a letter
- That there are **26** letters in the English alphabet, and letters are grouped in a certain order
- That letters represent **sounds of speech**
- That **words** are composed of letters and have meaning
- That one must be able to **correspond** letters and sounds to read

Development of Language Skills

Children learn language through interacting with others, by experiencing language in daily and relevant context, and through understanding that speaking and listening are necessary for effective communication. Teachers can promote **language development** by intensifying the opportunities a child has to experience and understand language.

Teachers can assist language development by:

- Modeling enriched vocabulary and teaching new words
- Using questions and examples to extend a child's descriptive language skills
- Providing ample response time to encourage children to practice speech
- Asking for clarification to provide students with the opportunity to develop communication skills
- Promoting conversations among children
- Providing feedback to let children know they have been heard and understood, and providing further explanation when needed

Relationship Between Oral and Written Language Development

Oral and written language development occur simultaneously. The acquisition of skills in one area supports the acquisition of skills in the other. However, oral language is not a prerequisite to written language. An immature form of oral language development is babbling, and an immature form of written language development is scribbling. **Oral language development** does not occur naturally, but does occur in a social context. This means it is best to include children in conversations rather than simply talk at them. **Written language development** can occur without direct instruction. In fact, reading and writing do not necessarily need to be taught through formal lessons if the child is exposed to a print-rich environment. A teacher can assist a child's language development by building on what the child already knows, discussing relevant and meaningful events and experiences, teaching vocabulary and literacy skills, and providing opportunities to acquire more complex language.

Print-Rich Environment

A teacher can provide a **print-rich environment** in the classroom in a number of ways. These include:

- **Displaying** the following in the classroom:
    - Children's names in print or cursive
    - Children's written work
    - Newspapers and magazines

- Instructional charts
- Written schedules
- Signs and labels
- Printed songs, poems, and rhymes

- Using **graphic organizers** such as KWL charts or story road maps to:
  - Remind students about what was read and discussed
  - Expand on the lesson topic or theme
  - Show the relationships among books, ideas, and words
- Using **big books** to:
  - Point out features of print, such as specific letters and punctuation
  - Track print from left to right
  - Emphasize the concept of words and the fact that they are used to communicate

Benefits of Print and Book Awareness

Print and book awareness helps a child understand:

- That there is a **connection** between print and messages contained on signs, labels, and other print forms in the child's environment
- That reading and writing are ways to obtain information and communicate ideas
- That **print** written in English runs from left to right and from top to bottom
- That a book has **parts**, such as a title, a cover, a title page, and a table of contents
- That a book has an **author** and contains a **story**
- That **illustrations** can carry meaning
- That **letters and words** are different
- That **words and sentences** are separated by spaces and punctuation
- That different **text forms** are used for different functions
- That print represents **spoken language**
- How to **hold** a book

Decoding

Decoding is the method or strategy used to make sense of printed words and figure out how to correctly pronounce them. In order to **decode**, a student needs to know the relationships between letters and sounds, including letter patterns; that words are constructed from phonemes and phoneme blends; and that a printed word represents a word that can be spoken. This knowledge will help the student recognize familiar words and make informed guesses about the pronunciation of unfamiliar words. Decoding is not the same as comprehension. It does not require an understanding of the meaning of a word, only a knowledge of how to recognize and pronounce it. Decoding can also refer to the skills a student uses to determine the meaning of a **sentence**. These skills include applying knowledge of vocabulary, sentence structure, and context.

Review Video: Phonics (Encoding and Decoding)
Visit mometrix.com/academy and enter code: 821361

Role of Fluency in Literacy Development

Fluency is the goal of literacy development. It is the ability to read accurately and quickly. Evidence of fluency includes the ability to recognize words automatically and group words for comprehension. At this point, the student no longer needs to decode words except for complex, unfamiliar ones. He or she is able to move to the next level and understand the **meaning** of a text.

The student should be able to self-check for comprehension and should feel comfortable expressing ideas in writing. Teachers can help students build fluency by continuing to provide:

- Reading experiences and discussions about text that gradually increase in level of difficulty
- Reading practice, both silently and out loud
- Word analysis practice
- Instruction on reading comprehension strategies
- Opportunities to express responses to readings through writing

Review Video: Fluency
Visit mometrix.com/academy and enter code: 531179

Role of Vocabulary in Literacy Development

When students do not know the meaning of words in a text, their comprehension is limited. As a result, the text becomes boring or confusing. The larger a student's **vocabulary** is, the better their reading comprehension will be. A larger vocabulary is also associated with an enhanced ability to **communicate** in speech and writing. It is the teacher's role to help students develop a good working vocabulary. Students learn most of the words they use and understand by listening to the world around them (adults, other students, media, etc.) They also learn from their reading experiences, which include being read to and reading independently. Carefully designed activities can also stimulate vocabulary growth, and should emphasize useful words that students see frequently, important words necessary for understanding text, and difficult words and phrases, such as idioms or words with more than one meaning.

Teaching Techniques Promoting Vocabulary Development

A student's **vocabulary** can be developed by:

- Calling upon a student's **prior knowledge** and making comparisons to that knowledge
- **Defining** a word and providing multiple examples of the use of the word in context
- Showing a student how to use **context clues** to discover the meaning of a word
- Providing instruction on **prefixes**, **roots**, and **suffixes** to help students break a word into its parts and decipher its meaning
- Showing students how to use a **dictionary and a thesaurus**
- Asking students to **practice** new vocabulary by using the words in their own writing
- Providing a **print-rich environment** with a word wall
- Studying a group of words related to a **single subject**, such as farm words, transportation words, etc. so that concept development is enhanced

Affixes, Prefixes, and Root Words

Affixes are syllables attached to the beginning or end of a word to make a derivative or inflectional form of a word. Both prefixes and suffixes are affixes. A **prefix** is a syllable that appears at the beginning of a word that creates a specific meaning in combination with the root or base word. For example, the prefix *mis* means wrong. When combined with the root word *spelling*, the word *misspelling* is created, which means wrong spelling. A **root word** is the base of a word to which affixes can be added. For example, the prefix *in-* or *pre-* can be added to the latin root word *vent* to create *invent* or *prevent*, respectively. The suffix *-er* can be added to the root word *manage* to create *manager*, which means one who manages. The suffix *-able*, meaning capable of, can be added to *manage* to create *managable*, which means capable of being managed.

Suffixes

A **suffix** is a syllable that appears at the end of a word that creates a specific meaning in combination with the root or base word. There are three types of suffixes:

- **Noun suffixes**—Noun suffixes can change a verb or adjective to a noun. They can denote the act of, state of, quality of, or result of something. For example, *-ment* added to *argue* becomes *argument*, which can be understood as the act the act of resulting state from arguing or the reasons given to prove an idea. Noun suffixes can also denote the doer, or one who acts. For example, *-eer* added to *auction* becomes *auctioneer*, meaning one who auctions. Other examples include *-hood*, *-ness*, *-tion*, *-ship*, and *-ism*.
- **Verb suffixes**—These change other words to verbs and denote to make or to perform the act of. For example, *-en* added to *soft* makes *soften*, which means to make soft. Other verb suffixes are *-ate* (perpetuate), *-fy* (dignify), and *-ize* (sterilize).
- **Adjectival suffixes**—These suffixes change other words to adjectives and include suffixes such as *-ful*, which means full of. When added to *care*, the word *careful* is formed, which means full of care. Other examples are *-ish* and *-less*.

Strategies to Improve Reading Comprehension

Teachers can model the strategies students can use on their own to better comprehend a text through a read-aloud. First, the teacher should do a walk-through of the story **illustrations** and ask, "What's happening here?" The teacher should then ask students to **predict** what the story will be about based on what they have seen. As the book is read, the teacher should ask open-ended questions such as, "Why do you think the character did this?" and "How do you think the character feels?" The teacher should also ask students if they can **relate** to the story or have background knowledge of something similar. After the reading, the teacher should ask the students to **retell** the story in their own words to check for comprehension. Possible methods of retelling include performing a puppet show or summarizing the story to a partner.

Review Video: The Link Between Grammar Skills and Reading Comprehension
Visit mometrix.com/academy and enter code: 411287

Role of Prior Knowledge in Determining Appropriate Literacy Education

Even preschool children have some literacy skills, and the extent and type of these skills have implications for instructional approaches. **Comprehension** results from relating two or more pieces of information. One piece comes from the text, and another piece might come from **prior knowledge** (something from a student's long-term memory). For a child, that prior knowledge comes from being read to at home; taking part in other literacy experiences, such as playing computer or word games; being exposed to a print-rich environment at home; and observing parents' reading habits. Children who have had **extensive literacy experience** are better prepared to further develop their literacy skills in school than children who have not been read to, have few books or magazines in their homes, are seldom exposed to high-level oral or written language activities, and seldom witness adults engaged in reading and writing. Children with a scant literacy background are at a disadvantage. The teacher must not make any assumptions about their prior knowledge, and should use intense, targeted instruction. Otherwise, the student may have trouble improving their reading comprehension.

> **Review Video: Importance of Promoting Literacy in the Home**
> Visit mometrix.com/academy and enter code: 862347

Second Language Acquisition of English

Theories of Language Development

Four theories of language development are:

- **Learning approach**—This theory assumes that language is first learned by imitating the speech of adults. It is then solidified in school through drills about the rules of language structures.
- **Linguistic approach**—Championed by Noam Chomsky in the 1950s, this theory proposes that the ability to use a language is innate. This is a biological approach rather than one based on cognition or social patterning.
- **Cognitive approach**—Developed in the 1970s and based on the work of Piaget, this theory states that children must develop appropriate cognitive skills before they can acquire language.
- **Sociocognitive approach**—In the 1970s, some researchers proposed that language development is a complex interaction of linguistic, social, and cognitive influences. This theory best explains the lack of language skills among children who are neglected, have uneducated parents, or live in poverty.

Classroom Practices Benefiting Second Language Acquisition

Since some students may have a limited understanding of English, a teacher should employ the following practices to promote second language acquisition:

- Make all instruction as **understandable** as possible and use simple and repeated terms.
- Relate instruction to the **cultures** of ESL children.
- Increase **interactive activities** and use gestures or nonverbal actions when modeling.
- Provide language and literacy development instruction in **all curriculum areas**.
- Establish **consistent routines** that help children connect words and events.
- Use a **schedule** so children know what will happen next and will not feel lost.
- Integrate ESL children into **group activities** with non-ESL children.
- Appoint bilingual students to act as **student translators**.
- Explain actions as activities happen so that a **word to action relationship** is established.
- Initiate opportunities for ESL children to **experiment** with and practice new language.
- Employ multisensory learning.

Teaching Strategies to Promote Listening Skills of ESL Students

Listening is a critical skill when learning a new language. Students spend a great deal more time listening than they do speaking, and far less time reading and writing than speaking. One way to encourage ESL students to listen is to talk about topics that are of **interest** to the ESL learner. Otherwise, students may tune out the speaker because they don't want to put in that much effort to learn about a topic they find boring. Another way to encourage ESL students to listen is to talk about content or give examples that are **easy** to understand or are **related** to a topic that is familiar to ESL students. Culturally relevant materials will be more interesting to ESL students, will make them feel more comfortable, and will contain vocabulary that they may already be familiar with.

Considerations Relevant to ESL Students Related to Learning by Listening

Listening is not a passive skill, but an **active** one. Therefore, a teacher needs to make the listening experience as rewarding as possible and provide as many auditory and visual clues as possible. Three ways that the teacher can make the listening experience rewarding for ESL students are:

- Avoid **colloquialisms** and **abbreviated or slang terms** that may be confusing to the ESL listener, unless there is enough time to define them and explain their use.
- Make the spoken English understandable by stopping to **clarify** points, **repeating** new or difficult words, and **defining** words that may not be known.
- Support the spoken word with as many **visuals** as possible. Pictures, diagrams, gestures, facial expressions, and body language can help the ESL learner correctly interpret the spoken language more easily and also leaves an image impression that helps them remember the words.

Top-Down and Bottom-Up Processing

ESL students need to be given opportunities to practice both top-down and bottom-up processing. If they are old enough to understand these concepts, they should be made aware that these are two processes that affect their listening comprehension. In **top-down processing**, the listener refers to **background and global knowledge** to figure out the meaning of a message. For example, when asking an ESL student to perform a task, the steps of the task should be explained and accompanied by a review of the vocabulary terms the student already understands so that the student feels comfortable tackling new steps and new words. The teacher should also allow students to ask questions to verify comprehension. In **bottom-up processing**, the listener figures out the meaning of a message by using "**data**" obtained from what is said. This data includes sounds (stress, rhythm, and intonation), words, and grammatical relationships. All data can be used to make conclusions or interpretations. For example, the listener can develop bottom-up skills by learning how to detect differences in intonation between statements and questions.

Listening Lessons

All students, but especially ESL students, can be taught **listening** through specific training. During listening lessons, the teacher should guide students through three steps:

- **Pre-listening activity**—This establishes the purpose of the lesson and engages students' background knowledge. This activity should ask students to think about and discuss something they already know about the topic. Alternatively, the teacher can provide background information.
- **The listening activity**—This requires the listener to obtain information and then immediately do something with that information. For example, the teacher can review the schedule for the day or the week. In this example, students are being given information about a routine they already know, and need to be able to identify names, tasks, and times.
- **Post-listening activity**—This is an evaluation process that allows students to judge how well they did with the listening task. Other language skills can be included in the activity. For example, this activity could involve asking questions about who will do what according to the classroom schedule (Who is the lunch monitor today?) and could also involve asking students to produce whole sentence replies.

Helping ESL Students Understand Subject Matter

Speaking

To help ESL students better understand subject matter, the following teaching strategies using spoken English can be used:

- **Read aloud** from a textbook, and then ask ESL students to **verbally summarize** what was read. The teacher should assist by providing new words as needed to give students the opportunity to practice vocabulary and speaking skills. The teacher should then read the passage again to students to verify accuracy and details.
- The teacher could ask ESL students to explain why the subject matter is important to them and where they see it fitting into their lives. This verbalization gives them speaking practice and helps them relate to the subject.
- Whenever small group activities are being conducted, ESL students can be placed with **English-speaking students**. It is best to keep the groups to two or three students so that the ESL student will be motivated by the need to be involved. English-speaking students should be encouraged to include ESL students in the group work.

Reading

There are supplemental printed materials that can be used to help ESL students understand subject matter. The following strategies can be used to help ESL students develop English reading skills.

- Make sure all ESL students have a **bilingual dictionary** to use. A thesaurus would also be helpful.
- Try to keep **content area books** written in the ESL students' native languages in the classroom. Students can use them side-by-side with English texts. Textbooks in other languages can be ordered from the school library or obtained from the classroom textbook publisher.
- If a student lacks confidence in his or her ability to read the textbook, the teacher can read a passage to the student and have him or her **verbally summarize** the passage. The teacher should take notes on what the student says and then read them back. These notes can be a substitute, short-form, in-their-own-words textbook that the student can understand.

General Teaching Strategies to Help ESL Students

Some strategies can help students develop more than one important skill. They may involve a combination of speaking, listening, and viewing. Others are mainly classroom management aids. General teaching strategies for ESL students include:

- **Partner** English-speaking students with ESL students as study buddies and ask the English-speaking students to share notes.
- Encourage ESL students to ask **questions** whenever they don't understand something. They should be aware that they don't have to be able to interpret every word of text to understand the concept.
- Dictate **key sentences** related to the content area being taught and ask ESL students to write them down. This gives them practice in listening and writing, and also helps them identify what is important.
- **Alternate** difficult and easy tasks so that ESL students can experience academic success.
- Ask ESL students to **label** objects associated with content areas, such as maps, diagrams, parts of a leaf, or parts of a sentence. This gives students writing and reading experience and helps them remember key vocabulary.

Chapter Quiz

Ready to see how well you retained what you just read? Scan the QR code to go directly to the chapter quiz interface for this study guide. If you're using a computer, simply visit the bonus page at **mometrix.com/bonus948/megaeemc073074** and click the Chapter Quizzes link.

Social Studies

Transform passive reading into active learning! After immersing yourself in this chapter, put your comprehension to the test by taking a quiz. The insights you gained will stay with you longer this way. Scan the QR code to go directly to the chapter quiz interface for this study guide. If you're using a computer, simply visit the bonus page at **mometrix.com/bonus948/megaeemc073074** and click the Chapter Quizzes link.

US History

Colonial Period (1607-1765)

The **colonial period** describes a time in which several European countries attempted to settle and colonize the Americas to expand their territories. The earliest attempts to colonize were by Spain and France, who conquered and settled much of what are now the southern and central parts of the United States of America. In the process of colonizing the Americas, many Native American groups were displaced or killed by disease and territorial expansion. The main focus of the colonial period in what is now the United States is often placed on the **thirteen English colonies**, which were located on the east coast. The primary reasons for the English colonization in the Americas were in response to England's policy of mercantilism and colonists' desire to be free from **religious persecution**. **Mercantilism** in England required the colonies to provide raw materials to England to continue to grow and support the mother country while also limiting trade with other nations. The other primary motivation for settlement included escape from persecution by the Church of England toward Catholic and other religious groups.

The 13 Colonies

The **thirteen colonies** were a group of English colonies that were overtly similar in their political and religious beliefs. The thirteen colonies were comprised of:

New England Colonies:

- New Hampshire
- Massachusetts
- Rhode Island
- Connecticut

Chesapeake Bay Colonies:

- Virginia
- Maryland

Review Video: The English Colony of Virginia
Visit mometrix.com/academy and enter code: 537399

Middle Colonies:

- New York
- Pennsylvania
- New Jersey
- Delaware

SOUTHERN COLONIES:

- North Carolina
- South Carolina
- Georgia

Review Video: Southern Colonies
Visit mometrix.com/academy and enter code: 703830

FRENCH AND INDIAN WAR

The **French and Indian War** was essentially a war over territory between the English colonies and the French colonies. Rising competition between the English and French empires brought more British military support into the colonies, which created a stronger feeling of unity between the colonies and England than ever before. In 1763, the **Treaty of Paris** brought an end to the war, as France relinquished some of its Eastern territory to England, including the territory east of modern-day Louisiana all the way to the Great Lakes. In the aftermath of the war, **tensions** rose between the colonies and England because of unequal investment in the war. British taxpayers had supplied the majority of funding for the war, while the colonists were forced to fight in a war that served the monarchy's interests rather than their own interests. These tensions, along with continued British occupation, were the foundation for the coming revolution.

AMERICAN REVOLUTION (1765-1783)

THE INTOLERABLE ACTS

Following the French and Indian War, Britain increased taxes and continued to impose quartering on the colonies. The most famous of these included the Stamp Acts, the Tea Acts, and the Quartering Acts. The purpose of these laws was to force the colonies to be dependent on Britain, and to help restore the British economy following the wars of the previous years. These laws were known to the British as the **Coercive Acts**. In America, they were called the **Intolerable Acts,** due to the offensive nature of England's attempt to control and stifle the colonies. As tensions rose, members of the colonies began organizing rebellious protests, such as the Boston Tea Party, in response to particular tax laws that were passed. These inciting reasons and protests led up to the official start of the **American Revolution.**

IMPORTANT EVENTS AND GROUPS LEADING UP TO AMERICAN REVOLUTION

Over several years, various events and groups contributed to the rebellion that became a revolution:

- **Sons of Liberty** – This was the protest group headed by Samuel Adams that incited the Revolution.
- **Boston Massacre** – On March 5, 1770, British soldiers fired on a crowd and killed five people.
- **Committees of Correspondence** – These were set up throughout the colonies to transmit revolutionary ideas and create a unified response.
- **The Boston Tea Party** – On December 6, 1773, the Sons of Liberty, dressed as Mohawks, dumped tea into the harbor from a British ship to protest the tea tax. The harsh British response further aggravated the situation.
- **First Continental Congress** – This was held in 1774 to list grievances and develop a response, including boycotts. It was attended by all the colonies with the exception of Georgia.

- **The Shot Heard Round the World** – In April, 1775, English soldiers on their way to confiscate arms in Concord passed through Lexington, Massachusetts and met the colonial militia called the Minutemen. A fight ensued. In Concord, a larger group of Minutemen forced the British to retreat.

Review Video: The First and Second Continental Congress
Visit mometrix.com/academy and enter code: 835211

Original 13 Colonies and Major Turning Points of the Revolution

The original **13 colonies** were: Connecticut, Delaware, Georgia, Maryland, Massachusetts, New Hampshire, New Jersey, New York, North Carolina, Pennsylvania, Rhode Island, South Carolina, and Virginia. Delaware was the first state to ratify the **constitution**.

The major turning points of the American Revolution were:

- The actions of the **Second Continental Congress** – This body established the Continental Army and chose George Washington as its commanding general. They allowed printing of money and created government offices.
- "**Common Sense**" – Published in 1776 by Thomas Paine, this pamphlet calling for independence was widely distributed.
- The **Declaration of Independence** – Written by Thomas Jefferson, it was ratified on July 4, 1776 by the Continental Congress assembled in Philadelphia.
- **Alliance with France** – Benjamin Franklin negotiated an agreement with France to fight with the Americans in 1778.
- **Treaty of Paris** – Signaled the official end of the war in 1782, granted independence to the colonies, and gave them generous territorial rights.

Review Video: Declaration of Independence
Visit mometrix.com/academy and enter code: 256838

Review Video: Colonization of the Americas
Visit mometrix.com/academy and enter code: 438412

Founding of a Nation

Each of the colonies overthrew the British representation within their own colonies and established their own state constitutions. The newly formed 13 states, with the guidance and primary authorship of Thomas Jefferson, unanimously adopted the **Declaration of Independence,** which officially separated the colonies from British rule. Shortly thereafter, the **Second Continental Congress**, made up of state representatives, met together to ratify the **Articles of Confederation**, which was the original constitution for the United States of America, outlining how sovereignty would be shared among the states in the new country. With the assistance of the French, the Americans were able to fend off a large scale naval and military invasion from the British and secure their revolution.

Review Video: Who are the Founding Fathers?
Visit mometrix.com/academy and enter code: 704562

Confederation Period

The **Confederation Period** (1783-1788) was the period in US history directly following the American Revolution. The Articles of Confederation held the states loosely, and the states were largely self-governing and did not have much political unity. In this format, the federal government was very weak, with no chief executive or judicial system. The weak federal government was bound to continue degrading in unity and would eventually fail if left without reform. In 1787, political leaders met to write a new constitution with more thoroughly written policies that would establish federal powers, while still sharing power with the state governments. This new constitution ended the confederation period and led the way into the Federalist Era.

Federalist Era (1788-1801)

The 1787 convention that wrote the new **Constitution of the United States of America** established three government branches, the **legislative** (making laws) the **executive** (enforcing laws), and the **judicial** (interpreting and judging laws). Having three branches with separate powers helped to provide what is known as **checks and balances** in government, so that no one branch will have too much power. This was meant to maintain liberty and state powers, while giving the federal government enough power to effectively govern the new country. The new constitution also established voting practices on the individual and state level, including the controversial topic of slavery and voting practices for states that did not abolish slavery. At this point, some northern states had made slavery illegal, but the constitution of the time allowed for the states to determine their own laws on the matter. The Federalist Era placed more power in the hands of the federal government, but also established a place for political parties to advocate for the rights of the people.

Bill of Rights and Amendments

Over the next few years, the need for revision to the constitution was made clear. In 1789, congress adopted several **amendments** to the constitution, mostly dealing with individual rights, such as the right to freedom of speech, the right to bear arms, and several others. The first ten amendments are called "**The Bill of Rights**." In the process of instituting these amendments, it was also laid out that any declarations (such as rights or laws) not specifically granted in the constitution or amendments to the constitution are reserved for the states or lower jurisdictions to establish.

Jeffersonian Era (1801-1817)

The **Jeffersonian Era** is defined by the influences of Thomas Jefferson and his political activism. In the Federalist Era, many of the political voices advocated for power going to those with wealth and property, rather than the equal rights of all people. Jefferson's political outlook was called **American Republicanism** (now the Democratic-Republican Party), which opposed aristocracy, elitism, and corruption in government. During Jefferson's presidency, he made significant strides toward a more inclusive voting system. He also managed to purchase Louisiana from France at an extremely reasonable price, thus roughly doubling the size of the United States at the time. From 1812-1815, a war ensued between the United Kingdom and the United States due to the British cutting off trade routes and fostering hostility between the Native Americans and the United States. The war concluded with no changes to boundaries, leading to the beginning of the **Era of Good Feelings.**

Era of Good Feelings and the Jacksonian Era

The **Era of Good Feelings** (1817-1825) followed the Jeffersonian Era, and was marked by the collapse of the Federalist system. President James Monroe attempted to deter the partisan political system and prevent political parties from driving national politics. During the Era of Good Feelings, there was a **temporary sense of national security** and a **desire for unity** in America following the war of previous years. Following Monroe's presidency, votes were largely split between the two major parties of the time, the **Whigs** and the **Democrats**.

During the **Jacksonian Era** (1825-1849), **voting rights** were extended to most white men over 21 years old and revised other federal policies. The policy favored the idea of election by the "common man," which expanded voting rights, while continuing to deny rights to women, Native Americans and African Americans. This period also saw an increase in **expansionism**, encouraging territorial expansion to the west in the name of manifest destiny. During this period, issues of slavery were largely avoided at first, though they grew over the coming years, leading into the Civil War Era.

Civil War Era (1850-1865)

The **Civil War Era** began with continued push from the northern states to expand democratic rights to Black people. The constitution of the time allowed for slavery to be a state's right to determine and enforce. Eleven states (with two to join later) determined to secede from the United States of America and become their own nation. In these eleven states, slavery was a major mode and means for the economy, and despite the overt ethical issues with slavery, these southern states were adamant about maintaining their way of life. The official Confederacy was formed in 1861 and continued until the end of the civil war in 1865.

Reconstruction Era (1865-1877)

Reconstruction and 13th, 14th, and 15th Amendments

Reconstruction was the period from 1865 to 1877, during which the South was under strict control of the US government. In March, 1867, all state governments of the former Confederacy were terminated, and **military occupation** began. Military commanders called for constitutional conventions to reconstruct the state governments, to which delegates were to be elected by universal male suffrage. After a state government was in operation and the state had **ratified the 14th Amendment**, its representatives were admitted to Congress. Three constitutional amendments from 1865 to 1870, which tried to rectify the problems caused by slavery, became part of the Reconstruction effort. The **13th Amendment** declared slavery illegal. The **14th Amendment** made all persons born or naturalized in the country US citizens, and forbade any state to interfere with their fundamental civil rights. The **15th Amendment** made it illegal to deny individuals the right to vote on the grounds of race. In his 1876 election campaign, President **Rutherford B. Hayes** promised to withdraw troops from the South, and did so in 1877.

Major Changes in Industry in the Late 1800s

Important events during this time of enormous business growth and large-scale exploitation of natural resources include:

- **Industrialization** – Like the rest of the world, the United States' entry into the Industrial Age was marked by many new inventions and the mechanization of factories.
- **Railroad expansion** – The Transcontinental Railroad was built from 1865 to 1969. Railroad tracks stretched over 35,000 miles in 1865, but that distance reached 240,000 miles by 1910. The raw materials and manufactured goods needed for the railroads kept mines and factories very busy.
- **Gold and silver mining** – Mines brought many prospectors to the West from 1850 to about 1875, but mining corporations soon took over.
- **Cattle ranching** – This was a large-scale enterprise beginning in the late 1860s, but by the 1880s open ranges were being fenced and plowed for farming and pastures. Millions of farmers moved into the high plains, establishing the "Bread Basket," which was the major wheat growing area of the country.

GILDED AGE (1877-1895)

The **Gilded Age**, from the 1870s to 1890, was so named because of the enormous wealth and grossly opulent lifestyle enjoyed by a handful of powerful families. This was the time when huge mansions were built as summer "cottages" in Newport, Rhode Island, and great lodges were built in mountain areas for the pleasure of families such as the Vanderbilts, Ascots, and Rockefellers.

Control of the major industries was held largely by the following men:

- Jay Gould—railroads
- Andrew Carnegie—steel
- John D. Rockefeller Sr.—oil
- Philip Danforth Armour—meatpacking
- J. P. Morgan—banking
- John Jacob Astor—fur pelts
- Cornelius Vanderbilt—steamboat shipping

These men were were known as **Robber Barons** for their ruthless business practices and exploitation of workers. Of course, all of these heads of industry diversified and became involved in multiple business ventures. To curb cutthroat competition, particularly among the railroads, and to prohibit restrained trade, Congress created the **Interstate Commerce Commission** and the **Sherman Anti-Trust Act**. Neither of these, however, was enforced.

Review Video: The Gilded Age: An Overview
Visit mometrix.com/academy and enter code: 684770

Review Video: The Gilded Age: Chinese Immigration
Visit mometrix.com/academy and enter code: 624166

IMMIGRATION TRENDS IN LATE 1800S

The population of the United States doubled between 1860 and 1890, with the arrival of 10 million immigrants. Most lived in the north. Cities and their **slums** grew tremendously because of immigration and industrialization. While previous immigrants had come from Germany, Scandinavia, and Ireland, the 1880s saw a new wave of immigrants from Italy, Poland, Hungary, Bohemia, and Greece, as well as Jewish groups from central and eastern Europe, especially Russia. The Roman Catholic population grew from 1.6 million in 1850 to 12 million in 1900, a growth that ignited an anti-Catholic backlash from the anti-Catholic Know-Nothing Party of the 1880s and the Ku Klux Klan. Exploited immigrant workers started **labor protests** in the 1870s, and the **Knights of Labor** was formed in 1878, calling for sweeping social and economic reform. Its membership reached 700,000 by 1886. Eventually, this organization was replaced by the **American Federation of Labor**, headed by Samuel Gompers.

PROGRESSIVE ERA (1896–1916)

The **Progressive Era**, which was the time period from the 1890s to the 1920s, got its name from progressive, reform-minded political leaders who wanted to export a just and rational social order to the rest of the world while increasing trade with foreign markets. Consequently, the United States interfered in a dispute between Venezuela and Britain. America invoked the **Monroe Doctrine** and sided with Cuba in its struggle for independence from Spain. The latter resulted in the **Spanish-American Wars** in 1898 that ended with Cuba, Puerto Rico, the Philippines, and Guam becoming American protectorates at the same time the United States annexed Hawaii. In 1900, America declared an **Open Door policy** with China to support its independence and open markets. In 1903, Theodore Roosevelt helped Panama become independent of Colombia, and then secured the right to build the **Panama Canal**. Roosevelt also negotiated the peace treaty to end the Russo-Japanese War, which earned him the Nobel Peace prize. He then sent the American fleet on a world cruise to display his country's power.

Review Video: The Progressive Era
Visit mometrix.com/academy and enter code: 722394

Domestic Accomplishments of the Progressive Era

To the Progressives, promoting law and order meant cleaning up city governments to make them honest and efficient, bringing more democracy and humanity to state governments, and establishing a core of social workers to improve slum housing, health, and education. Also during the **Progressive Era**, the national government strengthened or created the following regulatory agencies, services, and acts to oversee business enterprises:

- Passed in 1906, the **Hepburn A**ct reinforced the Interstate Commerce Commission. In 1902, Roosevelt used the Justice Department and lawsuits to try to break monopolies and enforce the **Sherman Anti-Trust Act**. The **Clayton Anti-Trust Act** was added in 1914.
- From 1898 to 1910, the **Forest Service** guided lumber companies in the conservation and more efficient use of woodland resources under the direction of Gifford Pinchot.
- In 1906, the **Pure Food and Drug Act** was passed to protect consumers from fraudulent labeling and adulteration of products.
- In 1913, the **Federal Reserve System** was established to supervise banking and commerce. In 1914, the **Fair Trade Commission** was established to ensure fair competition.

World War I (1917–1919)

When World War I broke out in 1914, America declared **neutrality**. The huge demand for war goods by the Allies broke a seven-year industrial stagnation and gave American factories full-time work. The country's sympathies lay mostly with the Allies, and before long American business and banking were heavily invested in an Allied victory. In 1916, **Woodrow Wilson** campaigned on the slogan "He kept us out of war." However, when the British ship the ***Lusitania*** was torpedoed in 1915 by a German submarine and many Americans were killed, the United States broke its neutrality and directly entered the war. Eventually, when it was proven that Germany was trying to incite Mexico and Japan into attacking the United States, Wilson declared war in 1917, even though America was unprepared. Nonetheless, America quickly armed and transferred sufficient troops to Europe, bringing the **Allies** to victory in 1918.

Review Video: WWI Overview
Visit mometrix.com/academy and enter code: 659767

Roaring Twenties and the Great Depression

The **Roaring Twenties** (1920–1929) refers to the economically successful period of time following World War I. New technologies such as automobiles, new forms of media such as films, and new communication technology became widely available. In the wake of industrial growth and revolution, culture shifted toward more modern sentiments, and moved toward a more **practical** approach to life. New forms of art and music were born and thrived during this period, and during this timeframe civil rights were expanded to allow **women to vote**. In 1929, the stock market crashed and caused the end of the Roaring Twenties and the beginning of the **Great Depression**, which lasted from 1930 until 1941. The Great Depression was characterized by high unemployment rates and a slow-moving market with little profit to be made. Many banks failed during this time, and there was no governmental protection against bank failures. As a result, many depositors withdrew their money from banks to protect themselves, removing much of the money from the economy in an effect called economic contraction.

World War II (1939–1945)

World War II began in 1939. As with World War I, the United States tried to stay out of World War II, even though the **Lend-Lease program** transferred munitions to Great Britain. However, on December 7, 1941, Japan attacked **Pearl Harbor** in Hawaii. Since Japan was an ally of Germany, the United States declared war on all the Axis powers. Although there was fighting in both Europe and the Pacific, the decision was made to concentrate on defeating Hitler first. Since it did not have combat within its borders, the United States became the great manufacturer of goods and munitions for the war effort. Women went to work in the factories, while the men entered the military. All facets of American life were centered on the war effort, including rationing, metal collections, and buying war bonds. The benefit of this production was an **end to the economic depression**. The influx of American personnel and supplies eventually brought victory in Europe in April of 1945, and in Asia the following August.

Review Video: World War II
Visit mometrix.com/academy and enter code: 759402

Major Programs and Events Resulting from the Cold War

After World War II, the Soviet Union kept control of Eastern Europe, including half of Germany. **Communism** spread around the world. Resulting fears led to:

- The **Truman Doctrine** (1947) – This was a policy designed to protect free peoples everywhere against oppression.
- The **Marshall Plan** (1948) – This devoted $12 billion to rebuild Western Europe and strengthen its defenses.
- The **Organization of American States** (1948) – This was established to bolster democratic relations in the Americas.
- The **Berlin Blockade** (1948-49) – The Soviets tried to starve out West Berlin, so the United States provided massive supply drops by air.
- The **North Atlantic Treaty Organization** (1949) – This was formed to militarily link the United States and western Europe so that an attack on one was an attack on both.
- The **Korean War** (1950-53) – This divided the country into the communist North and the democratic South.
- The **McCarthy era** (1950-54) – Senator Joseph McCarthy of Wisconsin held hearings on supposed Communist conspiracies that ruined innocent reputations and led to the blacklisting of suspected sympathizers in the government, Hollywood, and the media.

Major Events of the 1960s

The 1960s were a tumultuous time for the United States. Major events included:

- The **Cuban Missile Crisis** (1961) – This was a stand-off between the United States and the Soviet Union over a build-up of missiles in Cuba. Eventually, the Soviets stopped their shipments and a nuclear war was averted.
- The **assassinations** of President Kennedy (1963), Senator Robert Kennedy (1968), and Dr. Martin Luther King, Jr. (1968).
- The **Civil Rights Movement** – Protest marches were held across the nation to draw attention to the plight of Black citizens. From 1964 to 1968, race riots exploded in more than 100 cities.

- The **Vietnam War** (1964-73) – This resulted in a military draft. There was heavy involvement of American personnel and money. There were also protest demonstrations, particularly on college campuses. At Kent State, several students died after being shot by National Guardsmen.
- **Major legislation** – Legislation passed during this decade included the Civil Rights Act, the Clean Air Act, and the Water Quality Act. This decade also saw the creation of the Peace Corps, Medicare, and the War on Poverty, in which billions were appropriated for education, urban redevelopment, and public housing.

Presidents and Vice Presidents from 1972 to 1974

In a two-year time span, the United States had two presidents and two vice presidents. This situation resulted first from the resignation of Vice President **Spiro T. Agnew** in October of 1973 because of alleged kickbacks. President **Richard M. Nixon** then appointed House Minority Leader **Gerald R. Ford** to be vice president. This was accomplished through Senate ratification, a process that had been devised after Harry Truman succeeded to the presidency upon the death of Franklin Roosevelt and went through nearly four years of his presidency without a vice president. Nixon resigned the presidency in August of 1974 because some Republican party members broke into Democratic headquarters at the **Watergate** building in Washington, DC, and the president participated in covering up the crime. Ford succeeded Nixon, and had to appoint another vice president. He chose **Nelson Rockefeller**, former governor of New York.

Post-war Era and the Civil Rights Era

The **Post-War Era** (1945-1964) was a time of **economic recovery** and general growth in America. The wars of the past several decades inspired a more active foreign policy to deter such violent wars from occurring again. This largely focused on the Soviet Union and the expansion of Communism around the world. Several countries at this time participated in both a space race and an **arms race**, a rush to develop and accumulate more powerful weapons, particularly nuclear weapons, to become the world's strongest military power. The political differences and concerns over powerful armaments eventually led to the Cold War, Vietnam War, and Korean War. The 60s were also a major pivot-point for civil rights, leading into the **Civil Rights Era** (1965-1980). Due to the protesting and activism of several groups, including **Dr. Martin Luther King Jr**. and the **NAACP**, civil rights landmarks were made regarding racial equality, including laws dealing with **segregation**, **employment opportunity**, and **voting** rights.

Reagan Era (1981–1991)

The **Reagan Era** is an era largely describing the foreign policy of the United States during the 1980s and sometimes viewed as extending through the 1990s or early-2000s. During this period, conservative reforms worked to **increase military spending** while also **cutting taxes** and reducing or restricting the involvement of the national government. Ronald Reagan's financial policy revolved around the idea that if the government stepped back, the economy could grow, which would in turn help to reduce national debt.

1990s and Early-2000s

The 1990s and early-2000s were characterized largely by new economic developments surrounding the availability of computers and the development of the internet, allowing new technology to drive the economy in new ways. The economy boomed in the late 1990s leading into the early 2000s. Amid all of the economic success, the United States faced attacks by terrorist groups such as al-Qaeda, which caused alarm and greater restriction to national security and border control. The most influential of these terror attacks was the September 11, 2001 airliner hijacking, where al-Qaeda members took over four airplanes and used them as weapons to crash into key governmental and trade buildings. These attacks triggered a focus of American attention on terrorist groups, and led to several wars in Afghanistan and Iraq.

2008 to Present

Following the economic success of the 1990s and 2000s, the housing industry collapsed, leading to what is known as the **Great Recession** in 2008. In 2008, President Barack Obama was elected as the country's first African-American president. The war on terror continued until 2011, when Obama announced the death of Osama bin Laden, the al-Qaeda leader of the time. Obama's primary focus during his presidency included large stimulus packages and reforms to health insurance programs, an attempt to make healthcare affordable and available to all Americans. In 2016, President Donald Trump took office. His campaigns centered around immigration laws and tax reforms. Other major trends within this time period include a new wave of social equality issues surrounding same-sex rights and racial tension issues within America.

World History

Pre-Historical and Pre-Modern Periods

The earliest history of the human race is known as **pre-historical** due to the lack of record keeping. The earliest writing did not appear until the Sumerian civilization in Mesopotamia. In addition to the overt lack of writing from early civilizations, historical records were much more localized than more modern historical records. Ancient history can be broken down many ways, but a common distinction is the **pre-modern period**, including early civilizations such as Egypt, Babylon, and the Greek and Roman Empires. These early civilizations saw invention of technologies such as wood and early metalwork and the domestication of animals. Early civilizations were heavily dependent on agriculture and usually needed access to rivers for a consistent water source. The pre-modern period is viewed as ending with the connection of mainland Europe and some of Africa and Asia by the Greek and Roman Empires. The growth of these empires during this period also saw the worldwide spread of religions such as Judaism and Christianity.

Important Contributions of the Ancient Civilizations of Sumer, Egypt, and Indus Valley

These three ancient civilizations are distinguished by their unique contributions to the development of world civilization:

- **Sumer** used the first known writing system, which enabled the Sumerians to leave a sizeable written record of their myths and religion, advanced the development of the wheel and irrigation, and urbanized their culture.
- **Egypt** was united by the Nile River. Egyptians originally settled in villages on its banks, had a national religion that held their pharaohs as gods, had a central government that controlled civil and artistic affairs, and had writing and libraries.
- The **Indus Valley** was also called Harappan after the city of Harappa. This civilization started in the 3rd and 4th centuries BC and was widely dispersed over 400,000 square miles. It had a unified culture of luxury and refinement, no known national government, an advanced civic system, and prosperous trade routes.

Review Video: The Sumerians
Visit mometrix.com/academy and enter code: 939880

Review Video: Ancient Egypt
Visit mometrix.com/academy and enter code: 398041

Common Traits and Cultural Identifiers of the Early Empires of Mesopotamia, Egypt, Greece, and Rome

These empires all had: a strong military; a centralized government; control and standardization of commerce, money, and taxes; a weight system; and an official language.

- **Mesopotamia** had a series of short-term empires that failed because of their oppression of subject peoples.
- **Egypt** also had a series of governments after extending its territory beyond the Nile area. Compared to Mesopotamia, these were more stable and long-lived because they blended different peoples to create a single national identity.
- **Greece** started as a group of city-states that were united by Alexander the Great and joined to create an empire that stretched from the Indus River to Egypt and the Mediterranean coast. Greece blended Greek values with those of the local cultures, which collectively became known as Hellenistic society.
- **Rome** was an Italian city-state that grew into an empire extending from the British Isles across Europe to the Middle East. It lasted for 1,000 years and became the foundation of the Western world's culture, language, and laws.

Review Video: Ancient Greece
Visit mometrix.com/academy and enter code: 800829

Characteristics of Chinese and Indian Empires

While the Chinese had the world's longest lasting and continuous empires, the Indians had more of a cohesive culture than an empire system. Their distinct characteristics are as follows:

- **China** – Since the end of the Warring States period in 221 BC, China has functioned as an empire. Although the dynasties changed several times, the basic governmental structure remained the same into the 20th century. The Chinese also have an extensive written record of their culture which heavily emphasizes history, philosophy, and a common religion.
- **India** – The subcontinent was seldom unified in terms of government until the British empire controlled the area in the 19th and 20th centuries. In terms of culture, India has had persistent institutions and religions that have loosely united the people, such as the caste system and guilds. These have regulated daily life more than any government.

Middle Ages in European History

The **Middle Ages**, or Medieval times, was a period that ran from approximately 500-1500 AD. The fall of the Greek and Roman civilizations marks the beginning of this period, allowing for the rise of new independent countries, largely relying on the feudal system of government, with kings who allotted power and territory to governors. During this time, the centers of European civilization moved from the Mediterranean countries to France, Germany, and England, where strong national governments were developing. Key events of this time include:

- **Roman Catholicism** was the cultural and religious center of medieval life, extending into politics and economics.
- **Knights**, with their systems of honor, combat, and chivalry, were loyal to their king.
- **Peasants**, or serfs, served a particular lord and his lands.
- Many **universities** were established that still function in modern times.
- The **Crusades**, the recurring wars between European Christians and Middle East Muslims, raged over the Holy Lands.

- Charles the Great, or **Charlemagne**, created an empire across France and Germany around 800 AD.
- The **Black Death plague** swept across Europe from 1347-1350, leaving between one third and one half of the population dead.

> **Review Video: The Middle Ages**
> Visit mometrix.com/academy and enter code: 413133
>
> **Review Video: Trade in the Middle Ages**
> Visit mometrix.com/academy and enter code: 650839

Protestant Reformation

The dominance of the **Catholic Church** during the Middle Ages in Europe gave it immense power, which encouraged corrupt practices such as the selling of indulgences and clerical positions. The **Protestant Reformation** began as an attempt to reform the Catholic Church, but eventually led to separation from it. In 1517, Martin Luther posted his *Ninety-Five Theses* on the door of a church in Saxony, which criticized unethical practices, various doctrines, and the authority of the pope. Other reformers such as John Calvin and John Wesley soon followed, but disagreed among themselves and divided along doctrinal lines. Consequently, the Lutheran, Reformed, Calvinist, and Presbyterian churches were founded, among others. In England, King Henry VIII was denied a divorce by the pope, so he broke away and established the **Anglican Church**. The Protestant reformation caused the Catholic Church to finally reform itself, but the Protestant movement continued, resulting in a proliferation of new denominations.

Renaissance

Renaissance is the French word for rebirth, and is used to describe the renewal of interest in ancient Greek and Latin art, literature, and philosophy that occurred in Europe, especially Italy, from the 14th through the 16th centuries. Historically, it was also a time of great scientific inquiry, the rise of individualism, extensive geographical exploration, and the rise of secular values.

Notable figures of the Renaissance include:

- **Petrarch** – An Italian scholar, writer, and key figure in northern Italy, which is where the Renaissance started and where chief patrons came from the merchant class
- **Leonardo da Vinci** – Artist and inventor
- **Michelangelo** and **Raphael** – Artists
- **Desiderius Erasmus** – Applied historical scholarship to the New Testament and laid the seeds for the Protestant Reformation
- **Sir Thomas More** – A lawyer and author who wrote *Utopia*
- **Niccolò Machiavelli** – Author of *The Prince* and *Discourses*, which proposed a science of human nature and civil life
- **William Shakespeare** – A renowned playwright and poet

> **Review Video: Renaissance**
> Visit mometrix.com/academy and enter code: 123100

Age of Discovery and Colonialism

Throughout world history, there have been several waves of so-called **new imperialism**, in which established countries attempted to **colonize** territories that had not been explored by European nations. This was called the **Age of Discovery** largely because of the overseas exploration, "discovering" new lands, even though many of the explored lands were already populated. This colonialism was largely driven by the desire for increased wealth and resources, though many participants also sought after religious freedoms. Some of the earliest colonization attempts came from Spain and Portugal, who launched expeditions into Africa and Asia. These early colonial missions established the slave trade throughout Europe and for future colonial expansions. Later waves of colonialism included exploration of the **Americas** by Britain, France, and Spain. Other countries, such as China, Japan, and Russia, practiced imperialism in Asia. The process of colonizing many of these territories led to great injustices, such as the slave trade, and the horrific spread of disease and massacres of people groups such as the Aztecs in central Mexico and many Native American tribes in North America.

Decolonization

Following the powerful race for colonization throughout the world, many of the territories secured by European imperialism fought for their own **freedoms** and **independence**. Supporting these colonial missions was extremely costly and oftentimes, the colonials and the people from the ruling countries had very different priorities, which led to many disagreements. This was the case in the British colonies. Britain enacted many invasive and overcontrolling policies on the 13 established colonies. Tensions grew until the colonials revolted and declared their independence beginning the American Revolutionary War, which would solidify the United States of America as an independent nation. Several other countries worldwide followed suit and eventually secured their own independence. Decolonization largely began in the Americas and ended as late as 1960 in many African countries.

Worldwide Abolition of Slavery

Slavery has been accepted in various forms throughout most of known history. Contemporary to the decolonization period, the issue of slavery started to gain attention as an ethical matter worldwide. The movement to end slavery worldwide is known as **abolitionism** and roughly began in the late 1700s, however, anti-slavery sentiment was a slow-moving cause. The profitability of the slave trade and the use of slaves as the primary workforce for much of agriculture and shipping was a huge deterrent to change. In America, slavery was largely left as a states' right until tensions grew, leading into the American Civil War. Slavery was abolished progressively throughout the world, though at varying rates. Eventually, the United Nations adopted a firm doctrine on slavery, known as the Universal Declaration of Human Rights in 1948, which abolished slavery internationally.

Industrial Revolution

The **Industrial Revolution** started in England with the construction of the first **cotton mill** in 1733. Other inventions and factories followed in rapid succession. The **steel industry** grew exponentially when manufacturers realized that cheap, abundant English coal could be used instead of wood for melting metals. The **steam engine**, which revolutionized transportation and work power, came next. Around 1830, a factory-based, **technological era** was ushered into the rest of Europe. Society changed from agrarian to urban. A need for cheap, unskilled labor resulted in the extensive employment and abuse of women and children, who worked up to 14 hours a day, six days a week in deplorable conditions. Expanding populations brought crowded, unsanitary conditions to the cities, and the factories created air and water pollution. Societies had to deal with these new situations by enacting **child labor laws** and creating **labor unions** to protect the safety of workers.

Review Video: The Industrial Revolution
Visit mometrix.com/academy and enter code: 372796

Participants of World War I and World War II

World War I, which began in 1914, was fought by the **Allies** including Britain, France, Russia, Greece, Italy, Romania, and Serbia. They fought against the **Central Powers** of Germany, Austria-Hungary, Bulgaria, and Turkey. In 1917, the United States joined the Allies, and Russia withdrew to pursue its own revolution. World War I ended in 1918.

World War II was truly a world war, with fighting occurring on nearly every continent. Germany occupied most of Europe and Northern Africa. It was opposed by the countries of the British Empire, free France and its colonies, Russia, and various national resistance forces. Japan, an **Axis** ally of Germany, had been forcefully expanding its territories in Korea, China, Indonesia, the Philippines, and the South Pacific for many years. When Japan attacked Pearl Harbor in 1941, the United States joined the **Allied** effort. Italy changed from the Axis to the Allied side mid-war after deposing its own dictator. The war ended in Europe in April 1945, and in Japan in August 1945.

Importance of Cross-Cultural Comparisons in World History Instruction

It is important to make **cross-cultural comparisons** when studying world history so that the subject is **holistic** and not oriented to just Western civilization. Not only are the contributions of civilizations around the world important, but they are also interesting and more representative of the mix of cultures present in the United States. It is also critical to the understanding of world relations to study the involvement of European countries and the United States in international commerce, colonization, and development. **Trade routes** from ancient times linked Africa, Asia, and Europe, resulting in exchanges and migrations of people, philosophies, and religions, as well as goods. While many civilizations in the Americas thrived, and some became very sophisticated, many were eventually overcome or even erased by **European expansion**. The historic isolation of China and the modern industrialization of Japan have had huge impacts on their relations with the rest of the world. The more students understand this history and its effects on the modern world, the better they will able to function in their own spheres.

US Government and Citizenship

Principles of the Constitution

The six basic principles of the Constitution are:

1. **Popular Sovereignty** – The people establish government and give power to it; the government can function only with the consent of the people.
2. **Limited Government** – The Constitution specifies limits on government authority, and no official or entity is above the law.
3. **Separation of Powers** – Power is divided among three government branches: the legislative (Congress), the executive (President), and the judicial (federal courts).
4. **Checks and Balances** – This is a system that enforces the separation of powers and ensures that each branch has the authority and ability to restrain the powers of the other two branches, thus preventing tyranny.
5. **Judicial Review** – Judges in the federal courts ensure that no act of government is in violation of the Constitution. If an act is unconstitutional, the judicial branch has the power to nullify it.
6. **Federalism** – This is the division of power between the central government and local governments, which limits the power of the federal government and allows states to deal with local problems.

Classic Forms of Government

Forms of government that have appeared throughout history include:

- **Feudalism** – This is based on the rule of local lords who are loyal to the king and control the lives and production of those who work on their land.
- **Classical republic** – This form is a representative democracy. Small groups of elected leaders represent the interests of the electorate.
- **Absolute monarchy** – A king or queen has complete control of the military and government.
- **Authoritarianism** – An individual or group has unlimited authority. There is no system in place to restrain the power of the government.
- **Dictatorship** – Those in power are not held responsible to the people.
- **Autocracy** – This is rule by one person (despot), not necessarily a monarch, who uses power tyrannically.
- **Oligarchy** – A small, usually self-appointed elite rules a region.
- **Liberal democracy** – This is a government based on the consent of the people that protects individual rights and freedoms from any intolerance by the majority.
- **Totalitarianism** – All facets of the citizens' lives are controlled by the government.

Influences of Philosophers on Political Study

Ancient Greek philosophers **Aristotle** and **Plato** believed political science would lead to order in political matters, and that this scientifically organized order would create stable, just societies.

Thomas Aquinas adapted the ideas of Aristotle to a Christian perspective. His ideas stated that individuals have certain rights, but also certain duties, and that these rights and duties should determine the type and extent of government rule. In stating that laws should limit the role of government, he laid the groundwork for ideas that would eventually become modern constitutionalism.

Niccolò Machiavelli, author of *The Prince*, was a proponent of politics based solely on power.

Parliamentary and Democratic Systems of Government

In a **parliamentary system**, government involves a legislature and a variety of political parties. The head of government, usually a Prime Minister, is typically the head of the dominant party. A head of state can be elected, or this position can be taken by a monarch, such as in Great Britain's constitutional monarchy system.

In a **democratic system** of government, the people elect their government representatives. The term democracy is a Greek term that means "for the rule of the people." There are two forms of democracy—direct and indirect. In a direct democracy, each issue or election is decided by a vote where each individual is counted separately. An indirect democracy employs a legislature that votes on issues that affect large number of people whom the legislative members represent. Democracy can exist as a Parliamentary system or a Presidential system. The US is a presidential, indirect democracy.

Bill of Rights

The **United States Bill of Rights** was based on principles established by the **Magna Carta** in 1215, the 1688 **English Bill of Rights**, and the 1776 **Virginia Bill of Rights**. In 1791, the federal government added 10 amendments to the United States Constitution that provided the following **protections**:

- Freedom of speech, religion, peaceful assembly, petition of the government, and petition of the press
- The right to keep and bear arms
- No quartering of soldiers on private property without the consent of the owner
- Regulations on government search and seizure
- Provisions concerning prosecution
- The right to a speedy, public trial and the calling of witnesses
- The right to trial by jury
- Freedom from excessive bail or cruel punishment
- These rights are not necessarily the only rights
- Powers not prohibited by the Constitution are reserved to the states

Review Video: Bill of Rights
Visit mometrix.com/academy and enter code: 585149

Making a Formal Amendment to the Constitution

So far, there have been only **27 amendments** to the federal Constitution. There are four different ways to change the constitution: two methods for proposal and two methods for ratification:

1. An amendment is proposed by a two-thirds vote in each house of Congress and ratified by three-fourths of the state legislatures.
2. An amendment is proposed by a two-thirds vote in each house of Congress and ratified by three-fourths of the states in special conventions called for that purpose.
3. An amendment is proposed by a national convention that is called by Congress at the request of two-thirds of the state legislatures and ratified by three-fourths of the state legislatures.
4. An amendment is proposed by a national convention that is called by Congress at the request of two-thirds of the state legislatures and ratified by three-fourths of the states in special conventions called for that purpose.

Division of Powers

The **division of powers** in the federal government system is as follows:

- **National** – This level can coin money, regulate interstate and foreign trade, raise and maintain armed forces, declare war, govern United States territories and admit new states, and conduct foreign relations.
- **Concurrent** – This level can levy and collect taxes, borrow money, establish courts, define crimes and set punishments, and claim private property for public use.
- **State** – This level can regulate trade and business within the state, establish public schools, pass license requirements for professionals, regulate alcoholic beverages, conduct elections, and establish local governments.

There are three types of **delegated powers** granted by the Constitution:

1. **Expressed or enumerated powers** – These are specifically spelled out in the Constitution.
2. **Implied** – These are not expressly stated, but are reasonably suggested by the expressed powers.
3. **Inherent** – These are powers not expressed by the Constitution but ones that national governments have historically possessed, such as granting diplomatic recognition.

Powers can also be classified as reserved or exclusive. **Reserved powers** are not granted to the national government, but not denied to the states. **Exclusive powers** are those reserved to the national government, including concurrent powers.

Stages of Extending Suffrage in the US

Originally, the Constitution of 1789 provided the right to vote only to white male property owners. Through the years, suffrage was extended through the following five stages.

1. In the early 1800s, states began to eliminate **property ownership** and **tax payment qualifications**.
2. By 1810, there were no more **religious tests** for voting. In the late 1800s, the 15th Amendment protected citizens from being denied the right to vote because of **race or color**.
3. In 1920, the 19th Amendment prohibited the denial of the right to vote because of **gender**, and women were given the right to vote.
4. Passed in 1961 and ratified in 1964, the 23rd Amendment added the voters of the **District of Columbia** to the presidential electorate and eliminated the poll tax as a condition for voting in federal elections. The **Voting Rights Act of 1965** prohibited disenfranchisement through literacy tests and various other means of discrimination.
5. In 1971, the 26th Amendment set the minimum voting age at **18 years of age**.

Major Supreme Court Cases

Out of the many Supreme Court rulings, several have had critical historical importance. These include:

- **Marbury v. Madison** (1803) – This ruling established judicial review as a power of the Supreme Court.
- **Dred Scott v. Sandford** (1857) – This decision upheld property rights over human rights in the case of a slave who had been transported to a free state by his master, but was still considered a slave.
- **Brown v. Board of Education** (1954) – The Court ruled that segregation was a violation of the Equal Protection Clause and that the "separate but equal" practice in education was unconstitutional. This decision overturned the 1896 Plessy v. Ferguson ruling that permitted segregation if facilities were equal.
- **Miranda v. Arizona** (1966) – This ruling compelled the reading of Miranda rights to those arrested for crimes the law. It ensured that confessions could not be illegally obtained and that citizen rights to fair trials and protection under the law would be upheld.

Review Video: Marbury v. Madison
Visit mometrix.com/academy and enter code: 573964

Review Video: What was the Dred Scott Decision?
Visit mometrix.com/academy and enter code: 364838

Famous Speeches in US History that Defined Government Policy, Foreign Relations, and American Spirit

Among the best-known speeches and famous lines known to modern Americans are the following:

- The **Gettysburg Address** – Made by Abraham Lincoln on November 19, 1863, it dedicated the Gettysburg battleground's cemetery.
- The **Fourteen Points** – Made by Woodrow Wilson on January 18, 1918, this outlined Wilson's plans for peace and the League of Nations.
- **Address to Congress** – Made by Franklin Roosevelt on December 8, 1941, it declared war on Japan and described the attack on Pearl Harbor as "a day which will live in infamy."
- **Inaugural Address** – Made by John F. Kennedy on January 20, 1961, it contained the famous line: "Ask not what your country can do for you, ask what you can do for your country."
- **Berlin Address** – Made by John F. Kennedy on June 26, 1963, it contained the famous line "Ich bin ein Berliner," which expressed empathy for West Berliners in their conflict with the Soviet Union.
- "**I Have a Dream**" and "**I See the Promised Land**" – Made by Martin Luther King, Jr. on August 28, 1963 and April 3, 1968, respectively, these speeches were hallmarks of the Civil Rights Movement.
- **Brandenburg Gate speech** – Made by Ronald Reagan on June 12, 1987, this speech was about the Berlin Wall and the end of the Cold War. It contained the famous line "Tear down this wall."

Closed and Open Primaries in a Direct Primary System

The **direct primary system** is a means for members of a political party to participate in the selection of a candidate from their party to compete against the other party's candidate in a general election. A **closed primary** is a party nominating election in which only declared party members can vote. Party membership is usually established by registration. Currently, 26 states and the District of Columbia use this system. An **open primary** is a party nominating election in which any qualified voter can take part. The voter makes a public choice at the polling place about which primary to participate in, and the choice does not depend on any registration or previous choices. A **blanket primary**, which allowed voters to vote in the primaries of both parties, was used at various times by three states. The Supreme Court ruled against this practice in 2000.

Important Documents in United States History and Government

The following are among the greatest **American documents** because of their impact on foreign and domestic policy:

- Declaration of Independence (1776)
- The Articles of Confederation (1777)
- The Constitution (1787) and the Bill of Rights (1791)
- The Northwest Ordinance (1787)
- The Federalist Papers (1787-88)
- George Washington's Inaugural Address (1789) and Farewell Address (1796)
- The Alien and Sedition Act (1798)
- The Louisiana Purchase Treaty (1803)
- The Monroe Doctrine (1823); The Missouri Compromise (1830)
- The Compromise of 1850
- The Kansas-Nebraska Act (1854)

- The Homestead Act (1862)
- The Emancipation Proclamation (1863)
- The agreement to purchase Alaska (1866)
- The Sherman Anti-Trust Act (1890)
- Theodore Roosevelt's Corollary to the Monroe Doctrine (1905)
- The Social Security Act (1935) and other acts of the New Deal in the 1930s; The Truman Doctrine (1947); The Marshall Plan (1948)
- The Civil Rights Act (1964)

Federal Taxes

The four types of **federal taxes** are:

- **Income taxes on individuals** – This is a complex system because of demands for various exemptions and rates. Further, the schedule of rates can be lowered or raised according to economic conditions in order to stimulate or restrain economic activity. For example, a tax cut can provide an economic stimulus, while a tax increase can slow down the rate of inflation. Personal income tax generates about five times as much as corporate taxes. Rates are based on an individual's income, and range from 10 to 35 percent.
- **Income taxes on corporations** – The same complexity of exemptions and rates exists for corporations as individuals. Taxes can be raised or lowered according to the need to stimulate or restrain the economy.
- **Excise taxes** – These are taxes on specific goods such as tobacco, liquor, automobiles, gasoline, air travel, and luxury items, or on activities such as highway usage by trucks.
- **Customs duties** – These are taxes imposed on imported goods. They serve to regulate trade between the United States and other countries.

United States Currency System

The Constitution of 1787 gave the United States Congress the central authority to **print or coin money** and to **regulate its value**. Before this time, states were permitted to maintain separate currencies. The currency system is based on a **modified gold standard**. There is an enormous store of gold to back up United States currency housed at Fort Knox, Kentucky. Paper money is actually **Federal Reserve notes** and coins. It is the job of the Bureau of Engraving and Printing in the Treasury Department to design plates, special types of paper, and other security measures for bills and bonds. This money is put into general circulation by the Treasury and Federal Reserve Banks, and is taken out of circulation when worn out. Coins are made at the Bureau of the Mint in Philadelphia, Denver, and San Francisco.

Employment Act of 1946

The **Employment Act of 1946** established the following entities to combat unemployment:

- The **Council of Economic Advisers** (CEA) – Composed of a chair and two other members appointed by the President and approved by the Senate, this council assists the President with the development and implementation of US economic policy. The Council members and their staff, located in the Executive Office, are professionals in economics and statistics who forecast economic trends and provide analysis based on evidence-based research.
- The **Economic Report of the President** – This is presented every January by the President to Congress. Based on the work of the Council, the report recommends a program for maximizing employment, and may also recommend legislation.

- **Joint Economic Committee** (JEC) – This is a committee composed of 10 members of the House and 10 members of the Senate that makes a report early each year on its continuous study of the economy. Study is conducted through hearings and research, and the report is made in response to the president's recommendations.

Qualifications of a US Citizen

Anyone born in the US, born abroad to a US citizen, or who has gone through a process of **naturalization** to become a citizen, is considered a **citizen** of the United States. It is possible to lose US citizenship as a result of conviction of certain crimes such as treason. Citizenship may also be lost if a citizen pledges an oath to another country or serves in the military of a country engaged in hostilities with the US. A US citizen can also choose to hold dual citizenship, work as an expatriate in another country without losing US citizenship, or even renounce citizenship if he or she so chooses.

Rights, Duties, and Responsibilities Granted to or Expected from US Citizens

Citizens are granted certain rights under the US government. The most important of these are defined in the **Bill of Rights**, and include freedom of speech, religion, assembly, and a variety of other rights the government is not allowed to remove.

Duties of a US citizen include:

- Paying taxes
- Loyalty to the government, though the US does not prosecute those who criticize or seek to change the government
- Support and defend the Constitution
- Serve in the Armed Forces as required by law
- Obeying laws as set forth by the various levels of government.

Responsibilities of a US citizen include:

- Voting in elections
- Respecting one another's rights and not infringing upon them
- Staying informed about various political and national issues
- Respecting one another's beliefs

United States Political Systems

Representative Democracy

In a system of government characterized as a representative democracy, voters elect **representatives** to act in their interests. Typically, a representative is elected by and responsible to a specific subset of the total population of eligible voters; this subset of the electorate is referred to as a representative's constituency. A **representative democracy** may foster a more powerful legislature than other forms of government systems; to compensate for a strong legislature, most constitutions stipulate that measures must be taken to balance the powers within government, such as the creation of a separate judicial branch. Representative democracy became popular in post-industrial nations where increasing numbers of people expressed an interest in politics, but where technology and census counts remained incompatible with systems of direct democracy. Today, the majority of the world's population resides in representative democracies, including constitutional monarchies that possess a strong representative branch.

Democracy

Democracy, or rule by the people, is a form of government in which power is vested in the people and in which policy decisions are made by the majority in a decision-making process such as an election that is open to all or most citizens. Definitions of democracy have become more generalized and include aspects of society and political culture in democratic societies that do not necessarily represent a form of government. What defines a democracy varies, but some of the characteristics of a democracy could include the presence of a middle class, the presence of a civil society, a free market, political pluralism, universal suffrage, and specific rights and freedoms. In practice however, democracies do have limits on specific freedoms, which are justified as being necessary to maintain democracy and ensure democratic freedoms. For example, freedom of association is limited in democracies for individuals and groups that pose a threat to government or to society.

Presidential/Congressional System

In a **presidential system**, also referred to as a **congressional system**, the legislative branch and the executive branches are elected separately from one another. The features of a presidential system include a *president* who serves as both the head of state and the head of the government, who has no formal relationship with the legislative branch, who is not a voting member, who cannot introduce bills, and who has a fixed term of office. *Elections* are held at scheduled times. The president's *cabinet* carries out the policies of the executive branch and the legislative branch.

Political Parties

A **political party** is an organization that advocates a particular ideology and seeks to gain power within government. The tendency of members of political parties to support their party's policies and interests relative to those of other parties is referred to as partisanship. Often, a political party is comprised of members whose positions, interests and perspectives on policies vary, despite having shared interests in the general ideology of the party. As such, many political parties will have divisions within them that have differing opinions on policy. Political parties are often placed on a political spectrum, with one end of the spectrum representing conservative, traditional values and policies and the other end of the spectrum representing radical, progressive value and policies.

Types of Party Systems

There is a variety of **party systems**, including single-party systems, dominant-party systems, and dual-party systems. In a **single-party system**, only one political party may hold power. In this type of system, minor parties may be permitted, but they must accept the leadership of the dominant party. **Dominant-party systems** allow for multiple parties in opposition of one another, however the dominant party is the only party considered to have power. A **two-party system**, such as in the United States, is one in which there are two dominant political parties. In such a system, it is very difficult for any other parties to win an election. In most two-party systems, there is typically one right wing party and one left wing party.

Democratic Party

The **Democratic Party** was founded in 1792. In the United States, it is one of the two dominant political parties, along with the Republican Party. The Democratic Party is to the left of the Republican Party. The Democratic Party began as a conservative party in the mid-1800s, shifting to the left during the 1900s. There are many factions within the Democratic Party in the United States. The **Democratic National Committee (DNC)** is the official organization of the Democratic Party, and it develops and promotes the party's platform and coordinates fundraising and election strategies. There are Democratic committees in every US state and most US counties. The official symbol of the Democratic Party is the donkey.

Republican Party

The **Republican Party** is often referred to as the **GOP**, which stands for *Grand Old Party*. The Republican Party is considered socially conservative and economically neoliberal relative to the Democratic Party. Like the Democratic Party, there are factions within the Republic Party that agree with the party's overall ideology, but disagree with the party's positions on specific issues. The official symbol of the Republican Party is the elephant. The **Republican National Committee (RNC)** is the official organization of the Republican Party, and it develops and promotes the party's platform and coordinates fundraising and election strategies. There are Republican committees in every US state and most US counties.

Political Campaigns

A **political campaign** is an organized attempt to influence the decisions of a particular group of people. Examples of campaigns could include elections or efforts to influence policy changes. One of the first steps in a campaign is to develop a **campaign message**. The message must then be delivered to the individuals and groups that the campaign is trying to reach and influence through a campaign plan. There are various ways for a campaign to communicate its message to the intended audience, including public media; paid media such as television, radio and newspaper ads, billboards and the internet; public events such as protests and rallies; meetings with speakers; mailings; canvassing; fliers; and websites. Through these efforts, the campaign attempts to attract additional support and, ultimately, to reach the goal of the campaign.

Review Video: Political Campaigns
Visit mometrix.com/academy and enter code: 838608

Voting

Voting is a method of decision making that allows people to express their opinion or preference for a candidate or for a proposed resolution of an issue. In a democratic system, voting typically takes place as part of an **election**. An individual participates in the voting process by casting a vote, or a **ballot**; ballots are produced by states A *secret ballot* can be used at polls to protect voters' privacy. Individuals can also vote via *absentee ballot*. In some states voters can write-in a name to cast a vote for a candidate that is not on the ballot. Some states also use *straight ticket voting*, allowing the voter to vote for one party for all the elected positions on the ballot.

US Elections

In the United States, **officials** are elected at the federal, state and local levels. The first two articles of the Constitution, as well as various amendments, establish how **federal elections** are to be held. The **President** is elected indirectly, by electors of an electoral college. Members of the electoral college nearly always vote along the lines of the popular vote of their respective states. Members of **Congress** are directly elected. At the state level, state law establishes most aspects of how elections are held. There are many elected offices at the state level, including a governor and state legislature. There are also elected offices at the local level.

Voter Eligibility

The United States Constitution establishes that individual people are permitted to **vote** in elections if they are citizens of the United States and are at least eighteen years old. The **fifteenth** and **nineteenth amendments** of the United States Constitution stipulate that the right to vote cannot be denied to any United States citizen based on race or sex, respectively. States regulate voter eligibility beyond the minimum qualifications stipulated by the United States Constitution.

Depending on the regulations of individual states, individuals may be denied the right to vote if they are convicted criminals.

Advantages and Disadvantages to Two-Party System

Advocates of the **two-party system** argue that its advantages are that they are stable because they enable policies and government to change slowly rather than rapidly due to the relative lack of influence from small parties representing unconventional ideologies. In addition, they seem to drive voters toward a middle ground and are less susceptible to revolutions, coups, or civil wars. Among the critiques of the two-party system is the claim that stability in and of itself is not necessarily desirable, as it often comes at the expense of democracy. Critics also argue that the two-party system promotes negative political campaigns, in which candidates and their respective parties only take positions on issues that will differentiate themselves from their opponents, rather than focusing on policy issues that are of significance to citizens. Another concern is that if one of the two major parties becomes weak, a dominant-party system may develop.

Campaign Message

Political campaigns consist of three main elements, which are the campaign message, the money that is necessary to run the campaign, and the "machine," or the capital that is necessary to run the campaign. A campaign message is a succinct statement expressing why voters should support the campaign and the individual or policy associated with that campaign. The message is one of the most significant aspects of a political campaign, and a considerable amount of time, money and effort is invested in devising a successful campaign message, as it will be repeated throughout the campaign and will be one of the most identifying factors of the campaign.

Modern Election Campaigns in the US

Political campaigns in the US have changed and continue to change as advances in technology permit varied campaign methods. Campaigns represent a civic practice, and today they are a high profit industry. The US has an abundance of professional political consultants that employ highly sophisticated campaign management strategies and tools. The election process varies widely between the federal, state and local levels. Campaigns are typically controlled by individual candidates, rather than by the parties that they are associated with. Larger campaigns utilize a vast array of media to reach their targeted audiences, while smaller campaigns are typically limited to direct contact with voters, direct mailings and other forms of low-cost advertising to reach their audiences. In addition to fundraising and spending done by individual candidates, party committees and political action committees also raise money and spend it in ways that will advance the cause of the particular campaign they are associated with.

Voter Registration

Individuals have the responsibility of **registering to vote**. Every state except North Dakota requires citizens to register to vote. In an effort to increase voter turnout, Congress passed the **National Voter Registration Act** in 1993. This Act is also known as "Motor Voter," because it required states to make the voter registration process easier by providing registration services through drivers' license registration centers, as well as through disability centers, schools, libraries, and mail-in registration. Some states are exempt because they permit same-day voter registration, which enables voters to register to vote on the day of the election.

Presidential Elections

The President of the United States is elected **indirectly**, by members of an **electoral college**. Members of the electoral college nearly always vote along the lines of the popular vote of their respective states. The winner of a presidential election is the candidate with at least 270 electoral college votes. It is possible for a candidate to win the electoral vote, and lose the popular vote. Incumbent Presidents and challengers typically prefer a balanced ticket, where the President and Vice President are elected together and generally balance one another with regard to geography, ideology, or experience working in government. The nominated Vice Presidential candidate is referred to as the President's *running mate*.

Electoral College

Electoral college votes are cast by state by a group of electors; each elector casts one electoral college vote. State law regulates how states cast their electoral college votes. In all states except Maine and Nebraska, the candidate winning the most votes receives all the state's electoral college votes. In Maine and Nebraska two electoral votes are awarded based on the winner of the statewide election, and the rest go to the highest vote-winner in each of the state's congressional districts. Critics of the electoral college argue that it is undemocratic because the President is elected indirectly as opposed to directly, and that it creates inequality between voters in different states because candidates focus attention on voters in swing states who could influence election results. Critics argue that the electoral college provides more representation for voters in small states than large states, where more voters are represented by a single electoral than in small states and discriminates against candidates that do not have support concentrated in a given state.

Congressional Elections

Congressional elections are every two years. Members of the **House of Representatives** are elected for a two year term and elections occur every two years on the first Tuesday after November 1st in even years. A Representative is elected from each of the 435 House districts in the US House elections usually occur in the same year as Presidential elections. Members of the **Senate** are elected to six year terms; one-third of the Senate is elected every two years. Per the Seventeenth Amendment to the Constitution, which was passed in 1913, Senators are elected by the electorate of states. The country is divided into **Congressional districts**. Critics argue that this division eliminates voter choice, sometimes creating areas in which Congressional races are uncontested. Every ten years **redistricting** of Congressional districts occurs. However, redistricting is often partisan and therefore reduces the number of competitive districts. The division of voting districts resulting in an unfair advantage to one party in elections is known as gerrymandering. Gerrymandering has been criticized as being undemocratic.

State and Local Elections

State elections are regulated by state laws and constitutions. In keeping with the ideal of separation of powers, the legislature and the executive are elected separately at the state level, as they are at the federal level. In each state, a **Governor** and a **Lieutenant Governor** are elected. In some states, the Governor and Lieutenant Governor are elected on a joint ticket, while in other states they are elected separately from one another. In some states, executive positions such as Attorney General and Secretary of State are also elected offices. All members of state legislatures are elected, including state senators and state representatives. Depending on the state, members of the state supreme court and other members of the state judiciary may be chosen in elections. Local government can include the governments of counties and cities. At this level, nearly all government offices are filled through an election process. Elected local offices may include sheriffs, county school boards, and city mayors.

Campaign Finance and Independent Expenditures

An individual or group is legally permitted to make unlimited **independent expenditures** in association with federal elections. An independent expenditure is an expenditure that is made to pay for a form of communication that supports the election or defeat of a candidate; the expenditure must be made independently from the candidate's own campaign. To be considered independent, the communication may not be made with the cooperation or consultation with, or at the request or suggestion of, any candidate, any committees or political party associated with the candidate, or any agent that acts on behalf of the candidate. There are no restrictions on the amount that anyone may spend on an independent expenditure, however, any individual making an independent expenditure must report it and disclose the source of the funds they used.

Campaign Finance and Activities of Political Parties

Political parties participate in federal elections at the local, state and national levels. Most **party committees** must register with the **Federal Election Committee** and file reports disclosing federal campaign activities. While party committees may contribute funds directly to federal candidates, the amounts that they contribute are restricted by the campaign finance contribution limits. National and state party committees are permitted to make additional **coordinated expenditures**, within limits, to assist their nominees in general elections. However, national party committees are not permitted to make unlimited **independent expenditures**, also known as soft money, to support or oppose federal candidates. State and local party committees are also not permitted to use soft money for the purpose of supporting or opposing federal candidates, but they are allowed to spend soft money, up to a limit of $10,000 per source, on voter registration and on efforts aimed at increasing voter participation. All party committees are required to register themselves and file disclosure reports with the Federal Election Committee once their federal election activities exceed specified monetary limits.

Public Opinion

Public opinion represents the collective attitudes of individual members of the adult population in the United States of America. There are many varied forces that may influence public opinion. These forces include *public relations efforts* on the part of political campaigns and political parties. Another force affecting political opinion is the *political media* and the *mass media*. Public opinion is very important during elections, particularly Presidential elections, as it is an indicator of how candidates are perceived by the public and of how well candidates are doing during their election campaigns. Public opinion is often measured and evaluated using survey sampling.

Mass Media and Public Opinion

The **mass media** is critical in developing public opinion. In the short term people generally evaluate information they receive relative to their own beliefs; in the long term the media may have a considerable impact on people's beliefs. Due to the impact of the media on an individual's beliefs, some experts consider the effects of the media on an individual's independence and autonomy to be negative. Others view the impact of the media on individuals as a positive one, because the media provides information that expands worldviews and enriches lives, and fosters the development of opinions that are informed by many sources of information. A critical aspect of the relationship between the media and public opinion is who is in control of the knowledge and information that is disseminated through the media. Whoever controls the media can propagate their own agenda. The extent to which an individual interprets and evaluates information received through the media can influence behaviors such as voting patterns, consumer behavior, and social attitudes.

Economics

Effects Economy Can Have on Purchasing Decisions of Consumers

The **economy** plays an important role in how careful consumers are when using their resources. It also affects what they perceive as needs as opposed to what they perceive as wants. When the economy is doing well, unemployment figures are low, which means that people can easily attain their basic necessities. As a result, consumers are typically more willing to spend their financial resources. Consumers will also be more willing to spend their resources on products and services that are not necessary to their survival, but are instead products and services that they enjoy having and believe increase their quality of life. On the other hand, when the economy is in a slump, consumers are much more likely to cut back on their spending because they perceive a significantly higher risk of being unable to acquire basic necessities due to a lack of financial resources.

Common Terminology in Economics

- **Supply** is the amount of a product or service available to consumers.
- **Demand** is how much consumers are willing to pay for the product or service. These two facets of the market determine the price of goods and services. The higher the demand, the higher the price the supplier will charge; the lower the demand, the lower the price.
- **Scarcity** is a measure of supply. Demand is high when there is a scarcity, or low supply, of an item.
- **Choice** is related to scarcity and demand in that when an item in demand is scarce, consumers have to make difficult choices. They can pay more for an item, go without it, or go elsewhere for the item.
- **Money** is the cash or currency available for payment.
- **Resources** are the items one can barter in exchange for goods. Money is the cash reserves of a nation, while resources are the minerals, labor force, armaments, and other raw materials or assets a nation has available for trade.
- **Taxes** are legally required payments to the government for income, goods bought, or property owned. Taxes are categorized as direct or indirect.
- **Tariffs** are taxes specifically imposed on imports from another country.

Effects of Economic Downturn or Recession

When a **recession** happens, people at all levels of society feel the economic effects. For example:

- High **unemployment** results because businesses have to cut back to keep costs low, and may no longer have the work for the labor force they once did.
- **Mortgage rates** go up on variable-rate loans as banks try to increase their revenues, but the higher rates cause some people who cannot afford increased housing costs to sell or suffer foreclosure.
- **Credit** becomes less available as banks try to lessen their risk. This decreased lending affects business operations, home and auto loans, etc.
- **Stock market prices** drop, and the lower dividends paid to stockholders reduce their income. This is especially hard on retired people who rely on stock dividends.
- **Psychological depression and trauma** may occur in those who suffer bankruptcy, unemployment, or foreclosure during a depression.

Economic Effects of Abundant Natural Resources

The **positive economic aspects** of abundant natural resources are an increase in **revenue and new jobs** where those resources have not been previously accessed. For example, the growing demand for oil, gas, and minerals has led companies to venture into new regions.

The **negative economic aspects** of abundant natural resources are:

- **Environmental degradation**, if sufficient regulations are not in place to counter strip mining, deforestation, and contamination.
- **Corruption**, if sufficient regulations are not in place to counter bribery, political favoritism, and exploitation of workers as greedy companies try to maximize their profits.
- **Social tension**, if the resources are privately owned such that the rich become richer and the poor do not reap the benefits of their national resources. Class divisions become wider, resulting in social unrest.
- **Dependence**, if income from the natural resources is not used to develop other industries as well. In this situation, the economy becomes dependent on one source, and faces potential crises if natural disasters or depletion take away that income source.

Economics and Kinds of Economies

Economics is the study of the buying choices that people make, the production of goods and services, and how our market system works. The two kinds of economies are command and market. In a **command economy**, the government controls what and how much is produced, the methods used for production, and the distribution of goods and services. In a **market economy**, producers make decisions about methods and distribution on their own. These choices are based on what will sell and bring a profit in the marketplace. In a market economy, consumers ultimately affect these decisions by choosing whether or not to buy certain goods and services. The United States has a market economy.

Market Economy

The five characteristics of a **market economy** are:

- **Economic freedom** – There is freedom of choice with respect to jobs, salaries, production, and price.
- **Economic incentives** – A positive incentive is to make a profit. However, if the producer tries to make too high a profit, the consequences might be that no one will purchase the item at that price. A negative incentive would be a drop in profits, causing the producer to decrease or discontinue production. A boycott, which might cause the producer to change business practices or policies, is also a negative economic incentive.
- **Competition** – There is more than one producer for any given product. Consumers thereby have choices about what to buy, which are usually made based on quality and price. Competition is an incentive for a producer to make the best product at the best price. Otherwise, producers will lose business to the competition.
- **Private ownership** – Production and profits belong to an individual or to a private company, not to the government.
- **Limited government** – Government plays no role in the economic decisions of its individual citizens.

Factors of Production and Types of Markets That Create Economic Flow

The factors of **production** are:

- **Land** – This includes not only actual land, but also forests, minerals, water, etc.
- **Labor** – This is the work force required to produce goods and services, including factors such as talent, skills, and physical labor.

- **Capital** – This is the cash and material equipment needed to produce goods and services, including buildings, property, tools, office equipment, roads, etc.
- **Entrepreneurship** – Persons with initiative can capitalize on the free market system by producing goods and services.

The two types of markets are factor and product markets. The **factor market** consists of the people who exchange their services for wages. The people are sellers and companies are buyers. The **product market** is the selling of products to the people who want to buy them. The people are the buyers and the companies are the sellers. This exchange creates a circular economic flow in which money goes from the producers to workers as wages, and then flows back to producers in the form of payment for products.

Economic Impact of Technology

At the start of the 21st century, the role of **information and communications technologies** (ICT) grew rapidly as the economy shifted to a knowledge-based one. Output is increasing in areas where ICT is used intensively, which are service areas and knowledge-intensive industries such as finance; insurance; real estate; business services; health care; environmental goods and services; and community, social, and personal services. Meanwhile, the economic share for manufacturers is declining in medium- and low-technology industries such as chemicals, food products, textiles, gas, water, electricity, construction, and transport and communication services. Industries that have traditionally been high-tech, such as aerospace, computers, electronics, and pharmaceuticals are remaining steady in terms of their economic share. Technology has become the strongest factor in determining **per capita income** for many countries. The ease of technology investments as compared to industries that involve factories and large labor forces has resulted in more foreign investments in countries that do not have natural resources to call upon.

Geography

Geography

Geography involves learning about the world's primary **physical and cultural patterns** to help understand how the world functions as an interconnected and dynamic system. Combining information from different sources, geography teaches the basic patterns of climate, geology, vegetation, human settlement, migration, and commerce. Thus, geography is an **interdisciplinary** study of history, anthropology, and sociology. **History** incorporates geography in discussions of battle strategies, slavery (trade routes), ecological disasters (the Dust Bowl of the 1930s), and mass migrations. Geographic principles are useful when reading **literature** to help identify and visualize the setting, and also when studying **earth science**, **mathematics** (latitude, longitude, sun angle, and population statistics), and **fine arts** (song, art, and dance often reflect different cultures). Consequently, a good background in geography can help students succeed in other subjects as well.

Themes of Geography

The five themes of geography are:

- **Location** – This includes relative location (described in terms of surrounding geography such as a river, sea coast, or mountain) and absolute location (the specific point of latitude and longitude).
- **Place** – This includes physical characteristics (deserts, plains, mountains, and waterways) and human characteristics (features created by humans, such as architecture, roads, religion, industries, and food and folk practices).

- **Human-environmental interaction** – This includes human adaptation to the environment (using an umbrella when it rains), human modification of the environment (building terraces to prevent soil erosion), and human dependence on the environment for food, water, and natural resources.
- **Movement** –Interaction through trade, migration, communications, political boundaries, ideas, and fashions.
- **Regions** – This includes formal regions (a city, state, country, or other geographical organization as defined by political boundaries), functional regions (defined by a common function or connection, such as a school district), and vernacular regions (informal divisions determined by perceptions or one's mental image, such as the "Far East").

Review Video: Regional Geography
Visit mometrix.com/academy and enter code: 350378

Areas Covered by Geography

Geography is connected to many issues and provides answers to many everyday questions. Some of the areas covered by geography include:

- Geography investigates global climates, landforms, economies, political systems, human cultures, and migration patterns.
- Geography answers questions not only about where something is located, but also why it is there, how it got there, and how it is related to other things around it.
- Geography explains why people move to certain regions (climate, availability of natural resources, arable land, etc.).
- Geography explains world trade routes and modes of transportation.
- Geography identifies where various animals live and where various crops and forests grow.
- Geography identifies and locates populations that follow certain religions.
- Geography provides statistics on population numbers and growth, which aids in economic and infrastructure planning for cities and countries.

Physical and Cultural Geography and Physical and Political Locations

- **Physical geography** is the study of climate, water, and land and their relationships with each other and humans. Physical geography locates and identifies the earth's surface features and explores how humans thrive in various locations according to crop and goods production.
- **Cultural geography** is the study of the influence of the environment on human behaviors as well as the effect of human activities such as farming, building settlements, and grazing livestock on the environment. Cultural geography also identifies and compares the features of different cultures and how they influence interactions with other cultures and the earth.
- **Physical location** refers to the placement of the hemispheres and the continents.
- **Political location** refers to the divisions within continents that designate various countries. These divisions are made with borders, which are set according to boundary lines arrived at by legal agreements.

Both physical and political locations can be precisely determined by geographical surveys and by latitude and longitude.

Spatial Organization

Spatial organization in geography refers to how things or people are grouped in a given space anywhere on earth. Spatial organization applies to the **placement of settlements**, whether hamlets, towns, or cities. These settlements are located to make the distribution of goods and services convenient. For example, in farm communities, people come to town to get groceries, to attend church and school, and to access medical services. It is more practical to provide these things to groups than to individuals. These settlements, historically, have been built close to water sources and agricultural areas. Lands that are topographically difficult, have few resources, or experience extreme temperatures do not have as many people as temperate zones and flat plains, where it is easier to live. Within settlements, a town or city will be organized into commercial and residential neighborhoods, with hospitals, fire stations, and shopping centers centrally located. All of these organizational considerations are spatial in nature.

Important Terms Related to Maps

The most important terms used when describing items on a map or globe are:

- **Latitude and longitude** – Latitude and longitude are the imaginary lines (horizontal and vertical, respectively) that divide the globe into a grid. Both are measured using the 360 degrees of a circle.
- **Coordinates** – These are the latitude and longitude measures for a place.
- **Absolute location** – This is the exact spot where coordinates meet. The grid system allows the location of every place on the planet to be identified.
- **Equator** – This is the line at 0° latitude that divides the earth into two equal halves called hemispheres.
- **Parallels** – This is another name for lines of latitude because they circle the earth in parallel lines that never meet.
- **Meridians** – This is another name for lines of longitude. The Prime Meridian is located at 0° longitude, and is the starting point for measuring distance (both east and west) around the globe. Meridians circle the earth and connect at the Poles.

Review Video: 5 Elements of any Map
Visit mometrix.com/academy and enter code: 437727

Types of Maps

- A **physical map** is one that shows natural features such as mountains, rivers, lakes, deserts, and plains. Color is used to designate the different features.
- A **topographic map** is a type of physical map that shows the relief and configuration of a landscape, such as hills, valleys, fields, forest, roads, and settlements. It includes natural and human-made features.
- A **topological map** is one on which lines are stretched or straightened for the sake of clarity, but retain their essential geometric relationship. This type of map is used, for example, to show the routes of a subway system.
- A **political map** uses lines for state, county, and country boundaries; points or dots for cities and towns; and various other symbols for features such as airports and roads.

Map Styles

There are three basic styles of maps:

- **Base maps** – Created from aerial and field surveys, base maps serve as the starting point for topographic and thematic maps.
- **Topographic maps** – These show the natural and human-made surface features of the earth, including mountain elevations, river courses, roads, names of lakes and towns, and county and state lines.

- **Thematic maps** – These use a base or topographic map as the foundation for showing data based on a theme, such as population density, wildlife distribution, hill-slope stability, economic trends, etc.

Scale is the size of a map expressed as a ratio of the actual size of the land (for example, 1 inch on a map represents 1 mile on land). In other words, it is the proportion between a distance on the map and its corresponding distance on earth. The scale determines the level of detail on a map. **Small-scale maps** depict larger areas, but include fewer details. **Large-scale maps** depict smaller areas, but include more details.

Time Zones

Time is linked to **longitude** in that a complete rotation of the Earth, or 360° of longitude, occurs every 24 hours. Each hour of time is therefore equivalent to 15° of longitude, or 4 minutes for each 1° turn. By the agreement of 27 nations at the 1884 International Meridian Conference, the time zone system consists of **24 time zones** corresponding to the 24 hours in a day. Although high noon technically occurs when the sun is directly above a meridian, calculating time that way would result in 360 different times for the 360 meridians. Using the 24-hour system, the time is the same for all locations in a 15° zone. The 1884 conference established the meridian passing through Greenwich, England, as the zero point, or **prime meridian**. The halfway point is found at the 180th meridian, a half day from Greenwich. It is called the **International Date Line**, and serves as the place where each day begins and ends on earth.

Cartography

Cartography is the art and science of **mapmaking**. Maps of local areas were drawn by the Egyptians as early as 1300 BC, and the Greeks began making maps of the known world in the 6th century BC. Cartography eventually grew into the field of geography. The first step in modern mapmaking is a **survey**. This involves designating a few key sites of known elevation as benchmarks to allow for measurement of other sites. **Aerial photography** is then used to chart the area by taking photos in sequence. Overlapping photos show the same area from different positions along the flight line. When paired and examined through a stereoscope, the cartographer gets a three-dimensional view that can be made into a **topographical map**. In addition, a field survey (on the ground) is made to determine municipal borders and place names. The second step is to compile the information and **computer-draft** a map based on the collected data. The map is then reproduced or printed.

Globe and Map Projections

A **globe** is the only accurate representation of the earth's size, shape, distance, and direction since it, like the earth, is **spherical**. The flat surface of a map distorts these elements. To counter this problem, mapmakers use a variety of "**map projections**," a system for representing the earth's curvatures on a flat surface through the use of a grid that corresponds to lines of latitude and longitude. Some distortions are still inevitable, though, so mapmakers make choices based on the map scale, the size of the area to be mapped, and what they want the map to show. Some projections can represent a true shape or area, while others may be based on the equator and therefore become less accurate as they near the poles. In summary, all maps have some distortion in terms of the shape or size of features of the spherical earth.

Types of Map Projections

There are three main types of map projections:

- **Conical** – This type of projection superimposes a cone over the sphere of the earth, with two reference parallels secant to the globe and intersecting it. There is no distortion along the standard parallels, but distortion increases further from the chosen parallels. A Bonne projection is an example of a conical projection, in which the areas are accurately represented but the meridians are not on a true scale.
- **Cylindrical** – This is any projection in which meridians are mapped using equally spaced vertical lines and circles of latitude (parallels) are mapped using horizontal lines. A Mercator's projection is a modified cylindrical projection that is helpful to navigators because it allows them to maintain a constant compass direction between two points. However, it exaggerates areas in high latitudes.
- **Azimuthal** – This is a stereographic projection onto a plane centered so that a straight line from the center to any other point represents the shortest distance. This distance can be measured to scale.

Review Video: Map Projections
Visit mometrix.com/academy and enter code: 327303

Hemispheres and Parallels on the World Map

The definitions for these terms are as follows:

- **Northern Hemisphere** – This is the area above, or north, of the equator.
- **Southern Hemisphere** – This is the area below, or south, of the equator.
- **Western Hemisphere** – This is the area between the North and South Poles. It extends west from the Prime Meridian to the International Date Line.
- **Eastern Hemisphere** – This is the area between the North and South Poles. It extends east from the Prime Meridian to the International Date Line.
- **North and South Poles** – Latitude is measured in terms of the number of degrees north and south from the equator. The North Pole is located at 90°N latitude, while the South Pole is located at 90°S latitude.
- **Tropic of Cancer** – This is the parallel, or latitude, 23½° north of the equator.
- **Tropic of Capricorn** – This is the parallel, or latitude, 23½° south of the equator. The region between these two parallels is the tropics. The subtropics is the area located between 23½° and 40° north and south of the equator.
- **Arctic Circle** – This is the parallel, or latitude, 66½° north of the equator.
- **Antarctic Circle** – This is the parallel, or latitude, 66½° south of the equator.

Review Video: Geographical Features
Visit mometrix.com/academy and enter code: 773539

GPS

Global Positioning System (GPS) is a system of satellites that orbit the Earth and communicate with mobile devices to pinpoint the mobile device's position. This is accomplished by determining the distance between the mobile device and at least three satellites. A mobile device might calculate a distance of 400 miles between it and the first satellite. The possible locations that are 400 miles from the first satellite and the mobile device will fall along a circle. The possible locations on Earth relative to the other two satellites will fall somewhere along different circles. The point on Earth at which these three circles intersect is the location of the mobile device. The process of determining position based on distance measurements from three satellites is called **trilateration**.

Physical and Cultural Features of Geographic Locations and Countries

Physical Features

- **Vegetation zones, or biomes** – Forests, grasslands, deserts, and tundra are the four main types of vegetation zones.
- **Climate zones** – Tropical, dry, temperate, continental, and polar are the five different types of climate zones. Climate is the long-term average weather conditions of a place.

Cultural Features

- **Population density** – This is the number of people living in each square mile or kilometer of a place. It is calculated by dividing population by area.
- **Religion** – This is the identification of the dominant religions of a place, whether Christianity, Hinduism, Judaism, Buddhism, Islam, Shinto, Taoism, or Confucianism. All of these originated in Asia.
- **Languages** – This is the identification of the dominant or official language of a place. There are 12 major language families. The Indo-European family (which includes English, Russian, German, French, and Spanish) is spoken over the widest geographic area, but Mandarin Chinese is spoken by the most people.

Geomorphology

The study of landforms is call **geomorphology** or physiography, a science that considers the relationships between *geological structures* and *surface landscape features*. It is also concerned with the processes that change these features, such as erosion, deposition, and plate tectonics. Biological factors can also affect landforms. Examples are when corals build a coral reef or when plants contribute to the development of a salt marsh or a sand dune. Rivers, coastlines, rock types, slope formation, ice, erosion, and weathering are all part of geomorphology. A **landform** is a landscape feature or geomorphological unit. These include hills, plateaus, mountains, deserts, deltas, canyons, mesas, marshes, swamps, and valleys. These units are categorized according to elevation, slope, orientation, stratification, rock exposure, and soil type. Landform elements include pits, peaks, channels, ridges, passes, pools, and plains. The highest order landforms are continents and oceans. Elementary landforms such as segments, facets, and relief units are the smallest homogenous divisions of a land surface at a given scale or resolution.

Oceans, Seas, Lakes, Rivers, and Canals

- **Oceans** are the largest bodies of water on earth and cover nearly 71% of the earth's surface. There are five major oceans: Atlantic, Pacific (largest and deepest), Indian, Arctic, and Southern (surrounds Antarctica).
- **Seas** are smaller than oceans and are somewhat surrounded by land like a lake, but lakes are fresh water and seas are salt water. Seas include the Mediterranean, Baltic, Caspian, Caribbean, and Coral.
- **Lakes** are bodies of water in a depression on the earth's surface. Examples of lakes are the Great Lakes and Lake Victoria.
- **Rivers** are a channeled flow of water that start out as a spring or stream formed by runoff from rain or snow. Rivers flow from higher to lower ground, and usually empty into a sea or ocean. Great rivers of the world include the Amazon, Nile, Rhine, Mississippi, Ganges, Mekong, and Yangtze.

- **Canals** are artificial waterways constructed by humans to connect two larger water bodies. Examples of canals are the Panama and the Suez.

Mountains, Hills, Foothills, Valleys, Plateaus, and Mesas

The definitions for these geographical features are as follows:

- **Mountains** are elevated landforms that rise fairly steeply from the earth's surface to a summit of at least 1,000-2,000 feet (definitions vary) above sea level.
- **Hills** are elevated landforms that rise 500-2,000 feet above sea level.
- **Foothills** are a low series of hills found between a plain and a mountain range.
- **Valleys** are a long depression located between hills or mountains. They are usually products of river erosion. Valleys can vary in terms of width and depth, ranging from a few feet to thousands of feet.
- **Plateaus** are elevated landforms that are fairly flat on top. They may be as high as 10,000 feet above sea level and are usually next to mountains.
- **Mesas** are flat areas of upland. Their name is derived from the Spanish word for table. They are smaller than plateaus and often found in arid or semi-arid areas.

Formation of Mountains

Mountains are formed by the movement of geologic plates, which are rigid slabs of rocks beneath the earth's crust that float on a layer of partially molten rock in the earth's upper mantle. As the plates collide, they push up the crust to form mountains. This process is called **orogeny**. There are three basic forms of orogeny:

- If the collision of continental plates causes the crust to buckle and fold, a chain of **folded mountains**, such as the Appalachians, the Alps, or the Himalayas, is formed.
- If the collision of the plates causes a denser oceanic plate to go under a continental plate, a process called **subduction**; strong horizontal forces lift and fold the margin of the continent. A mountain range like the Andes is the result.
- If an oceanic plate is driven under another oceanic plate, **volcanic mountains** such as those in Japan and the Philippines are formed.

Coral Reefs

Coral reefs are formed from millions of tiny, tube-shaped **polyps**, an animal life form encased in tough limestone skeletons. Once anchored to a rocky surface, polyps eat plankton and miniscule shellfish caught with poisonous tentacles near their mouth. Polyps use calcium carbonate absorbed from chemicals given off by algae to harden their body armor and cement themselves together in fantastic shapes of many colors. Polyps reproduce through eggs and larvae, but the reef grows by branching out shoots of polyps. There are three types of coral reefs:

- **Fringing reefs** – These surround, or "fringe," an island.
- **Barrier reefs** – Over the centuries, a fringe reef grows so large that the island sinks down from the weight, and the reef becomes a barrier around the island. Water trapped between the island and the reef is called a lagoon.
- **Atolls** – Eventually, the sinking island goes under, leaving the coral reef around the lagoon.

Plains, Deserts, Deltas, and Basins

- **Plains** are extensive areas of low-lying, flat, or gently undulating land, and are usually lower than the landforms around them. Plains near the seacoast are called lowlands.

- **Deserts** are large, dry areas that receive less than 10 inches of rain per year. They are almost barren, containing only a few patches of vegetation.
- **Deltas** are accumulations of silt deposited at river mouths into the seabed. They are eventually converted into very fertile, stable ground by vegetation, becoming important crop-growing areas. Examples include the deltas of the Nile, Ganges, and Mississippi River.
- **Basins** come in various types. They may be low areas that catch water from rivers; large hollows that dip to a central point and are surrounded by higher ground, as in the Donets and Kuznetsk basins in Russia; or areas of inland drainage in a desert when the water can't reach the sea and flows into lakes or evaporates in salt flats as a result. An example is the Great Salt Lake in Utah.

Marshes and Swamps and Tundra and Taiga

Marshes and swamps are both **wet lowlands**. The water can be fresh, brackish, or saline. Both host important ecological systems with unique wildlife. There are, however, some major differences. **Marshes** have no trees and are always wet because of frequent floods and poor drainage that leaves shallow water. Plants are mostly grasses, rushes, reeds, typhas, sedges, and herbs. **Swamps** have trees and dry periods. The water is very slow-moving, and is usually associated with adjacent rivers or lakes.

Both taiga and tundra regions have many plants and animals, but they have few humans or crops because of their harsh climates. **Taiga** has colder winters and hotter summers than tundra because of its distance from the Arctic Ocean. Taiga is the world's largest forest region, located just south of the tundra line. It contains huge mineral resources and fur-bearing animals. **Tundra** is a Russian word describing marshy plain in an area that has a very cold climate but receives little snow. The ground is usually frozen, but is quite spongy when it is not.

Humid Continental, Prairie, Subtropical, and Marine Climates

- A **humid continental climate** is one that has four seasons, including a cold winter and a hot summer, and sufficient rainfall for raising crops. Such climates can be found in the United States, Canada, and Russia. The best farmlands and mining areas are found in these countries.
- **Prairie climates**, or steppe regions, are found in the interiors of Asia and North America where there are dry flatlands (prairies that receive 10-20 inches of rain per year). These dry flatlands can be grasslands or deserts.
- **Subtropical climates** are very humid areas in the tropical areas of Japan, China, Australia, Africa, South America, and the United States. The moisture, carried by winds traveling over warm ocean currents, produces long summers and mild winters. It is possible to produce a continuous cycle of a variety of crops.
- A **marine climate** is one near or surrounded by water. Warm ocean winds bring moisture, mild temperatures year-round, and plentiful rain. These climates are found in Western Europe and parts of the United States, Canada, Chile, New Zealand, and Australia.

Adaptation to Environmental Conditions

The environment influences the way people live. People **adapt** to **environmental conditions** in ways as simple as putting on warm clothing in a cold environment; finding means to cool their surroundings in an environment with high temperatures; building shelters from wind, rain, and temperature variations; and digging water wells if surface water is unavailable. More complex adaptations result from the physical diversity of the earth in terms of soil, climate, vegetation, and topography. Humans take advantage of opportunities and avoid or minimize limitations. Examples of environmental limitations are that rocky soils offer few opportunities for agriculture and rough terrain limits accessibility. Sometimes, **technology** allows humans to live in areas that were once uninhabitable or undesirable. For example, air conditioning allows people to live comfortably in hot climates; modern heating systems permit habitation in areas with extremely low temperatures, as is the case with research facilities in Antarctica; and airplanes have brought people to previously inaccessible places to establish settlements or industries.

Natural Resources, Renewable Resources, Nonrenewable Resources, and Commodities

Natural resources are things provided by nature that have commercial value to humans, such as minerals, energy, timber, fish, wildlife, and the landscape. **Renewable resources** are those that can be replenished, such as wind, solar radiation, tides, and water (with proper conservation and clean-up). Soil is renewable with proper conservation and management techniques, and timber can be replenished with replanting. Living resources such as fish and wildlife can replenish themselves if they are not over-harvested. **Nonrenewable resources** are those that cannot be replenished. These include fossil fuels such as oil and coal and metal ores. These cannot be replaced or reused once they have been burned, although some of their products can be recycled. **Commodities** are natural resources that have to be extracted and purified rather than created, such as mineral ores.

Harmful or Potentially Harmful Interaction with Environment

Wherever humans have gone on the earth, they have made **changes** to their surroundings. Many are harmful or potentially harmful, depending on the extent of the alterations. Some of the changes and activities that can harm the **environment** include:

- Cutting into mountains by machine or blasting to build roads or construction sites
- Cutting down trees and clearing natural growth
- Building houses and cities
- Using grassland to graze herds
- Polluting water sources
- Polluting the ground with chemical and oil waste
- Wearing out fertile land and losing topsoil
- Placing communication lines cross country using poles and wires or underground cable
- Placing railway lines or paved roads cross country
- Building gas and oil pipelines cross country
- Draining wetlands
- Damming up or re-routing waterways
- Spraying fertilizers, pesticides, and defoliants
- Hunting animals to extinction or near extinction

Carrying Capacity and Natural Hazards

Carrying capacity is the maximum, sustained level of use of an environment can incur without sustaining significant environmental deterioration that would eventually lead to environmental destruction. Environments vary in terms of their carrying capacity, a concept humans need to learn to measure and respect before harm is done. Proper **assessment of environmental conditions** enables responsible decision making with respect to how much and in what ways the resources of a particular environment should be consumed. **Energy and water conservation** as well as recycling can extend an area's carrying capacity. In addition to carrying capacity limitations, the physical environment can also have occasional extremes that are costly to humans. **Natural hazards** such as hurricanes, tornadoes, earthquakes, volcanoes, floods, tsunamis, and some forest fires and insect infestations are processes or events that are not caused by humans, but may have serious consequences for humans and the environment. These events are not preventable, and their precise timing, location, and magnitude are not predictable. However, some precautions can be taken to reduce the damage.

Applying Geography to Interpretation of the Past

Space, environment, and chronology are three different points of view that can be used to study history. Events take place within **geographic contexts**. If the world is flat, then transportation choices are vastly different from those that would be made in a round world, for example. Invasions of Russia from the west have normally failed because of the harsh winter conditions, the vast distances that inhibit steady supply lines, and the number of rivers and marshes to be crossed, among other factors. Any invading or defending force anywhere must make choices based on consideration of space and environmental factors. For instance, lands may be too muddy or passages too narrow for certain equipment. Geography played a role in the building of the Panama Canal because the value of a shorter transportation route had to outweigh the costs of labor, disease, political negotiations, and equipment, not to mention a myriad of other effects from cutting a canal through an isthmus and changing a natural land structure as a result.

Applying Geography to Interpretation of the Present and Plans for the Future

The decisions that individual people as well as nations make that may **affect the environment** have to be made with an understanding of spatial patterns and concepts, cultural and transportation connections, physical processes and patterns, ecosystems, and the impact, or "footprint," of people on the physical environment. Sample issues that fit into these considerations are recycling programs, loss of agricultural land to further urban expansion, air and water pollution, deforestation, and ease of transportation and communication. In each of these areas, present and future uses have to be balanced against possible harmful effects. For example, wind is a clean and readily available resource for electric power, but the access roads to and noise of wind turbines can make some areas unsuitable for livestock pasture. Voting citizens need to have an understanding of **geographical and environmental connections** to make responsible decisions.

Historiography

Common Terminology Used When Studying History

When studying history, it is important to have a clear understanding of various terms that can be used interchangeably. The term **time** refers to the continuous passing of events in the past, present, and future. Time is a scientific measure that conventionally uses minutes, hours, days, and years as its **standard measures**. Time passes with or without significant events taking place. **History** is distinct from time as it is the record of **significant events** throughout the past. The term **chronology** refers to the arrangement of events in their correct order. As history contains uncertainty, the chronology of particular events is up for debate. Terms used to describe the ebb and flow of history are change and continuity. **Continuity** refers to periods of time that are relatively stable in history with no major changes, whereas times of **change** refer to rich periods in history with significant events that alter the common practices of that time, often leading into a new era. When describing what has changed for a civilization over time, it is common to focus on political, economic, social, and technological aspects. For instance, the United States government was established in 1776 and continues today. This demonstrates a change at the beginning of the timeline related the United States, but since then, there has been political continuity as it has existed for roughly 250 years. Other aspects of life in this period may have experienced other changes, such as the innovation of electricity, steam engines, and automobiles. When a portion of time has relatively stable conditions such that it can be summed up by a common characterization, it is called a **period of time**; this process of summing up time into periods is called **periodization**.

Civilization, City-States, and Empires

Since history is the study of recorded events throughout time, it is naturally tied to organized society with a developed language to record the events. The development necessary to record history generally coincides with early civilization. A **civilization** is a human society that has established complex means of surviving as a group. These **functions** are developing a food supply, a social structure, a shared language, a culture, and technology. The first known complex civilization is Mesopotamia, which was more easily developed due to its fertile farmlands, access to water through an available river. Mesopotamia is a good example of a **city-state**, which is essentially an independently sovereign city that does not depend on another government. Mesopotamia, as an early civilization, was the central hub and government in its region. The model of city-states still exists today, though they are often comparatively less significant in size and economy compared to other nation-states. Examples of modern city-states include Monaco, Vatican City, and Singapore. As the early civilizations continued to develop, they would eventually grow into **empires**, which are larger sovereign states with multiple territories, though they are usually governed centrally by a monarch or emperor.

Interpreting Timelines

Timelines are a useful tool for visualizing the chronology of events as well as a great method to map out periods and view changes or continuity throughout history. Timelines can focus on either small or large ranges and can be multifaceted so that one period or type of event can be compared with another. A key element of a timeline is having a consistent interval mapped out. For instance, if we wanted to construct a timeline to map the events that happened for a single day, we would likely use hours to plot out the continuum. One might start the timeline at 12am and end the timeline at 12am the next night to show the picture of the entire day. Each event or period, such as sleeping, waking up, eating, going to work, and special occurrences can be marked on the timeline to plot out the day. If someone wanted to compare multiple days, these timelines could be lined up and compared and contrasted to find what is common to all days and what is unique. These same concepts can be applied to historical timelines as well. Instead of mapping just one day, one might consider mapping the events leading up to and throughout a particular war. The significance of events should change with the focus of the timeline. Seeing events plotted on a steady continuum of time can be very helpful in understanding the pacing of events throughout history.

Relationships between Historical Events and their Implications

As one aspect of society changes, it frequently proves to have significant effects on other parts of society. One of the easiest ways to see this effect is the innovation of new technologies. An example of a highly impactful technology is the printing press. Prior to this invention, all written documents had to be written by hand, which was time-consuming and costly. Books were very expensive and rare, which put the burden of education on mainly religious authorities and very wealthy classes of people. This new innovation allowed for more written works to be spread, which caused a need for literacy and education, ultimately evoking huge cultural and political changes. Technology tends to be a much quicker influencer of change in civilization, as it is sudden and can have dramatic impacts on how things are done. Cultural, political, and economic effects tend to move more gradually but likewise have strong effects that can change civilization forever.

Primary and Secondary Sources of Historical Information

When studying history, it is important to consider the reliability, validity, and availability of sources of information. **Primary sources** are first-hand accounts of an event, such as a transcript of a speech, a recording, statistics, or a work of art. **Secondary sources** are indirect records, such as text books, newspapers, and other forms of reviews of the primary sources. Secondary sources of information can still be valid and useful, but are more open to **interpretation** and **bias**. Information from recent history, such as the election of a president in the 2010s is very reliable, as there are many sources of information that are in consensus about the objective event. Furthermore, many people still alive are primary sources since they were alive and witnessed the election. This is not true of less modern history, such as the election of Abraham Lincoln in 1860. There are still plentiful records of the information, but all witnesses to the election have passed away at this point. This event took place in an era where newspapers and legitimate documentation was widespread and available. The clarity and objectivity of sources are indisputable because they are so abundant. If, however, we only had political cartoons and election campaign brochures to go by, the reliability and accuracy of the information may be up for debate because the source materials are only secondary sources of information and are likely to contain biases. Generally, the further back in history one researches, the fewer sources are available due to lack of documentation, technological limitations, and language barriers. With fewer sources, and possibly conflicting information, historians must put together the most reasonable explanation of what took place during the period in question, given the amount of information available to them.

Types of Sources of Information Used in Historical Research

- **Almanacs**—books that are published each year to express current information for consideration in the coming year. These often act as time capsules for that particular year and can give historians insight into economic and technological details of the time.
- **Encyclopedias**—resources that cover a variety of topics broadly for the purpose of giving the reader an overview. Wikipedia is an internet-based version of an encyclopedia that is useful for finding leads or obtaining general information about a topic.
- **Bibliographies**—a list of resources used in composing a scholarly work. These are usually primary and secondary sources that can be used to check an author's sources or to give leads on similar research. Similar concepts include works-cited pages and literature reviews.
- **Periodical Guides**—a series of publications over time, usually in the form of magazines or journals. These usually broach a more specific category of information, such as on research methods, psychology, or medical procedures, and are intended to help members of a particular field stay up-to-date with current research in their field.
- **Biographical Dictionaries**—a resource that contains a list of important names to know about the given subject and a description of how they contributed to the field. For instance, if one were interested in the Revolutionary War, a biographical dictionary would include information on each of the founding fathers and other significant individuals of the time.
- **Maps**—representations of land and territories that can display a variety of factors, including geographical features, political features, economics, demographics, and many more aspects. Digital maps can generally be manipulated to show multiple features at once.

Uses and Limitations of Various Historical Source Materials

Historical source materials are a type of primary source material that offer historians the opportunity to study people, places, and events that occurred in the past. Unfortunately, there are limitations to what these materials can tell us. A limitation of **historical source materials** is that they may be biased by those who created them. For example, those who create historical documents such as letters may leave out details or exaggerate parts in order to make their points more convincing. Another limitation might be that some historical sources only provide evidence for certain points of view, as they were recorded by those with specific interests and perspectives.

- An **oral history** provides an account of an event that happened in the past, which is told by the person who was there when it happened. Oral histories are important because they allow us to learn about things that may not be written in books or recorded in documents.
- **Newspapers** are important source materials for scholars because they provide a detailed account of the past, which cannot be found in books or other sources. Newspapers are not always reliable as they may not be based on fact, while others might omit certain information or give undue weight towards one side of an issue at the expense of another.
- **Diaries** and personal **journals** can provide valuable information for historians because they are detailed histories of people's lives. However, the reliability of these accounts is always in question because they were created by just one person and aren't always written with the intention of sharing.
- **Artifacts** can be defined as objects created by humans, which can give hints at the peoples' material culture and intangible culture. Material culture includes things like buildings or furniture while intangible culture includes things like music or dance. The benefits of artifacts are that they can offer insights into how people lived in the past. They can also be used to shed light on the thoughts, feelings, fears, tensions, customs, rituals, and other social practices at that time.
- **Tax lists** and **census data** are useful sources of insight into how people lived during a certain time. They provide us with reliable information about the income, demographics, and beliefs of the people living in a particular time.
- **Personal correspondence** has been an important form of historical information for historians. It gives an insight into the lives and interactions of ordinary people. The main benefits of using personal correspondence as a source for history is that it provides an authentic portrayal of the author's thoughts and feelings during a time period or in response to significant events.

Historical Interpretation and Biases

History is a discipline that relies on the interpretation of **facts** to create **narratives**. Due to the types and availability of sources, history tends to leave itself open to **subjectivity**. Often, this means that **biases** are introduced at either the source of information, the interpretation of the information, or at the explanation of the information. For instance, if the only **sources of information** about an event are newspapers, the author of these historical sources may have been biased, causing the **interpretation** of the actual events to be skewed from the start. Similarly, the person interpreting the source may have their own biases that they introduce or even **teach** to others in the process of communicating the historical narrative. Commonly described biases in modern interpretation of history generally revolve around sociopolitical issues such as Eurocentrism, popular political parties, economic biases, and cultural favoritism.

Chapter Quiz

Ready to see how well you retained what you just read? Scan the QR code to go directly to the chapter quiz interface for this study guide. If you're using a computer, simply visit the bonus page at **mometrix.com/bonus948/megaeemc073074** and click the Chapter Quizzes link.

MEGA Practice Test

Want to take this practice test in an online interactive format?
Check out the bonus page, which includes interactive practice questions and much more: **mometrix.com/bonus948/megaeemc073074**

SCAN HERE

Reading/Language Arts

1. The pairs of words *sea* and *see*, *fair* and *fare*, are called:

a. Homophones
b. Antonyms
c. Homographs
d. Twin words

2. A syllable must contain:

a. A vowel
b. A consonant
c. Both a vowel and a consonant
d. A meaning

3. Public speakers want to give speeches that make their audience pay attention, but they also want to give speeches whose messages are meaningful enough to remain in audience member's minds. This can best be accomplished with:

a. Simple language and stories
b. Strict logical progression
c. Sophisticated language and ideas
d. Eye contact

4. The purpose of corrective feedback is:

a. To provide students with methods for explaining to the teacher or classmates what a passage was about
b. To correct an error in reading a student has made, specifically clarifying where and how the error was made so that the student can avoid similar errors in the future
c. To provide a mental framework that will help the student correctly organize new information
d. To remind students that error is essential in order to truly understand and that it is not something to be ashamed of

5. A cloze test evaluates a student's:

a. Reading fluency
b. Understanding of context and vocabulary
c. Phonemic skills
d. Ability to apply the alphabetic principle to previously unknown material

6. Tea/tee, stair/stare, and shoe/shoo are:

a. Homophones
b. Synonyms
c. Homographs
d. Homonyms

7. A student is able to apply strategies to comprehend the meanings of unfamiliar words; can supply definitions for words with several meanings such as *crucial, criticism,* and *witness*; and is able to reflect on her background knowledge in order to decipher a word's meaning. These features of effective reading belong to which category?

a. Word recognition
b. Vocabulary
c. Content
d. Comprehension

8. *Bi, re,* and *un* are:

a. Suffixes, appearing at the beginning of base words to change their meaning
b. Suffixes, appearing at the end of base words to enhance their meaning
c. Prefixes, appearing at the beginning of base words to emphasize their meaning
d. Prefixes, appearing at the beginning of base words to change their meanings

9. Of the following activities that promote building vocabulary for young children, which one is most dependent on the teacher?

a. Repeatedly singing the same familiar song over and over
b. Reciting the same familiar rhymes and chants repeatedly
c. Listening to repeated readings of the same favorite story
d. A word wall in the classroom to illustrate words/concepts

10. Reading and writing are usually seen as the two major aspects of literacy that are taught in the classroom. What critical aspect of literacy begins at home but is often neglected in the classroom?

a. oral language development
b. health information
c. math skills
d. science awareness

11. A teacher is trying to assist a student with his scientific vocabulary. The student is also an English Language Learner. What could the teacher suggest to help him improve his scientific vocabulary most effectively?

a. Use a glossary of scientific terms for each chapter of the textbook, and discuss these terms with the student as the relevant chapters are referenced.
b. Assign a specific number of scientific terms for the student to look up in a scientific dictionary and share with the class.
c. Explain the scientific terms to this student as concepts are presented and related experiments performed.
d. Ask the student to look for context to define difficult scientific words, and have the student record the definitions in a notebook.

12. A student is asked to use a similar word to describe someone who was happy. What type of word would this be?

a. An antonym
b. A homonym
c. A synonym
d. A euphemism

13. Homonyms such as *bare* and *bear* are similar in sound yet have different meanings. What would a teacher suggest a student do to avoid misusing these words?

a. Memorize the definitions of the difficult words.
b. Check a dictionary or thesaurus to verify a word's usage.
c. Avoid encountering difficult words.
d. Ignore being precise in the definition.

14. Where does a prefix appear in a word?

a. At the beginning
b. At the end
c. In the middle
d. Any place

15. Where does a suffix appear in a word?

a. at the beginning
b. at the end
c. in the middle
d. any place

16. Consider the following sentence:

Mary is a very gregarious person and has many friends.

Based on the context of this sentence, the word *gregarious* means:

a. shy.
b. angry.
c. friendly.
d. mean.

17. A knowledge of word elements can enable a student to understand the meanings of unfamiliar words. What does the prefix *circum-* mean in the word *circumference?*

a. beyond
b. after
c. around
d. before

18. What does the prefix *poly-* mean in the word *polygon*?

a. Few
b. Several
c. None
d. Many

19. A number of verb forms are used in headlines. These include simple tenses, infinitive forms, and auxiliary verbs dropped in the passive voice. Which headline below uses a simple tense?

a. LOST DOG RETURNS
b. GOVERNOR TO VISIT CITY
c. GRADUATE NAMED VALEDICTORIAN
d. HERO GIVEN AWARD

20. The English word *salary* has a 2,000-year-old etymology related to which of the following?

a. Salt
b. Celery
c. Money
d. Earnings

21. Which of the following is an example of a portmanteau?

a. Fax
b. Brunch
c. Babysitter
d. Saxophone

22. The English language word "quark" is an example of the result of which linguistic process?

a. Blending
b. Conversion
c. Neologisms
d. Onomatopoeia

23. A patient dies in surgery and the reporting doctor describes the death as a "negative patient outcome." This is best identified as an example of:

a. Jargon
b. Ambiguity
c. Euphemism
d. Connotation

24. Oral language development across the curriculum requires

a. teamwork.
b. planning.
c. cooperation.
d. all of the above.

25. A teacher asked his students to prepare a presentation that could be shown in a foreign country. He advised them to

a. use idioms.
b. avoid anecdotes local to the foreign country.
c. avoid quotes from a foreign national of the country.
d. keep the presentation simple and succinct.

26. Ross and Janine were discussing a magazine article about codes, ciphers, and steganography, which their teacher gave as a reading assignment. The article described steganography as the practice of embedding secret messages in other messages, pictures, or music, etc. Janine asked Ross to explain the word *embedded* to her. Here is the conversation they had:

Ross: Steganography is cool!
Janine (rolling her eyes): I've heard the word embedded used to describe reporters being put with the troops overseas, but what does it mean here?
Ross: It means the message is inserted into a bigger message.
Janine: But how does that make the message hard to see? You can see the embedded reporters with the troops on TV.
Ross: The writing or picture is too small to see, so it can be hidden. These messages aren't big like a person. That's why someone who needs to read the information has to use special tools to be able to see the secret message.
Janine: Oh, I understand.

What did Ross say that helped Janine finally understand what *embedded* meant with regard to steganography?

a. *Embedded* means removed into something.
b. *Embedded* means inserted and plainly visible in something.
c. *Embedded* means inserted and hidden in something.
d. *Embedded* means inserted in a foreign language in something.

27. President Lincoln's Gettysburg Address was about:

a. the future of America.
b. a dedication of lives lost on this battlefield.
c. an eloquent expression of democratic ideals.
d. all of the above.

28. Which type of nonverbal message deals with belonging, control, respect, or disapproval?

a. Emotive messages
b. Relational messages
c. Relationship messages
d. Interpersonal messages

29. Making a strong argument in a speech, conversation, or debate requires:

a. Forceful delivery
b. Acknowledging the opposing point of view with respect
c. Demonstrating the weakness of the opposing view with mockery
d. Seizing the floor when the opponent's point is strong
e. Seizing the floor when the opponent's point is weak

30. Metaphor, a rhetorical device, is used in oratory to:

a. Compare two distinct things using "like" or "as"
b. Surprise listeners
c. Introduce a new idea via a familiar one
d. Make the speech poetic and beautiful
e. Cause listeners to think philosophically

31. Interpersonal communications can be unclear due to all of the following except:

a. Misinterpretation
b. Assumptions
c. Environmental context
d. Relational context
e. Similar backgrounds of communicators

32. Which of the following statements regarding eye contact is false?

a. It suggests confidence and presence of mind.
b. It lends a humanizing sensibility to a speech.
c. Audience members are drawn into the presentation if the speaker makes repeated eye contact that lasts long enough to suggest emotional intimacy.
d. It sparks audience interest because the occasion of the speech seems, on some level, to be a conversation in which they are engaged.

33. Which of the following is the best definition of information literacy?

a. It is the set of skills required for reading and comprehending different information.
b. It is the cognitive skill set necessary to amass a comprehensive base of knowledge.
c. It is the skill set required for the finding, retrieval, analysis, and use of information.
d. It is the set of skills necessary for effectively communicating information to others.

34. When creating an outline, it is important to use:

a. Prepositions
b. Progressivism
c. Abbreviation
d. Subordination

35. Which of the basic elements of the writing process should be completed before the first draft is written?

a. Prewriting
b. Revising
c. Conferencing
d. Editing

36. A third-grade teacher decides to introduce new vocabulary words using a word association game. What is required in order for the students to succeed with word associations?

a. The definition of the new words
b. Prior knowledge
c. The spelling of the word
d. Synonyms of the new words

37. A classroom teacher observes that a new ELL student consistently omits the /h/ sound in words. Of these, what is the first factor the teacher should consider?

a. The student may have an articulation disorder.
b. The student may be a native Spanish speaker.
c. The student may need a hearing assessment.
d. The student may have a respiratory problem.

38. Examples of onomatopoeia are:

a. Sink, drink, mink, link
b. Their, there, they're
c. Drip, chirp, splash, giggle
d. Think, in, thin, ink

39. A third grader knows he needs to write from left to right and from top to bottom on the page. He knows what sounds are associated with specific letters. He can recognize individual letters and can hear word families. He correctly identifies prefixes, suffixes, and homonyms, and his reading comprehension is very good. However, when he is asked to write, he becomes very upset. He has trouble holding a pencil, his letters are very primitively executed, and his written work is not legible. He most likely has:

a. Dysgraphia
b. Dyslexia
c. Dyspraxia
d. Nonverbal learning disorder

40. A story about a young detective who solves mysteries using mental and physical skills would most likely be classified as which of the following?

a. Action and adventure
b. Historical fiction
c. Horror and ghost stories
d. Biography

41. An understanding of the meanings of prefixes and suffixes such as *dis, mis, un, re, able,* and *ment* are important for:

a. Reading comprehension
b. Word recognition
c. Vocabulary building
d. Reading fluency

42. Round-robin reading refers to the practice of allowing children to take turns reading portions of a text aloud to the rest of the group during class. Which of the following statements is <u>least</u> true about this practice?

a. Students have the chance to practice reading aloud with this strategy.
b. This practice is ineffective in its use of time, leaving students who are not reading aloud to become bored or daydream.
c. Round-robin reading lacks the creativity or engaging qualities that will interest students in building literacy skills.
d. This practice helps students feel comfortable with reading aloud due to continuous practice and encouragement from the teacher and peers.

43. A teacher has a student in her class who is not very motivated to write because he finds it difficult. She observes he has a highly visual learning style, does not like reading books but loves graphic novels, and has considerable artistic drawing talent and interest. Which of the following instructional strategies would best address his individual needs, strengths, and interests?

a. Giving him audio recordings to accompany and guide his writing homework
b. Letting him complete all assignments by drawing pictures instead of writing
c. Having him draw the pictures and write accompanying text in graphic novels
d. Providing and assigning him to view animated videos on the topic of writing

44. Which of the following gives an example of a fallacy of inconsistency?

a. "There are exceptions to all general statements."
b. "Please pass me; my parents will be upset if I fail."
c. "He is guilty: there is no evidence he is innocent."
d. "Have you stopped cheating on your assignments?"

45. A teacher wants to work on her students' listening comprehension in addition to their reading comprehension since she understands that the skills are interrelated. She has a series of short stories that she thinks the students will enjoy. Which of the following would be the best supplement to typical written comprehension exercises?

a. Preview the content and then read the stories aloud to the students. Assess listening comprehension through verbal and written questions.
b. Ask the students to choose one story each to read aloud to a small group. Encourage the students to discuss what they have learned afterward.
c. Assign each student a story to read and require them to write a report on it. Each student should then present his or her report based on what he or she has learned to the class.
d. Have the students read stories aloud to the class, and create mock tests based upon the main ideas which they identify.

46. Collaborative Strategic Reading (CSR) is a teaching technique that depends on two teaching practices. These practices are:

a. Cooperative learning and reading comprehension
b. Cooperative reading and metacognition
c. Reading comprehension and metacognition
d. Cooperative learning and metacognition

47. Young children are more likely to respond to analogies in stories rather than to metaphors because:

a. They are old enough to understand the abstract thinking and symbolism that analogies express.
b. The ability to understand the kinds of abstraction expressed in metaphors is not developed until later in childhood.
c. They can apply the concepts expressed in analogies to their own daily lives, but metaphors do not compare things that children are familiar with.
d. Metaphors and symbols are usually found only in books that children find boring because of their abstractions.

48. A class is reading a 14-line poem in iambic pentameter. There are three stanzas of four lines each, and a two-line couplet at the end. Words at the end of each line rhyme with another word in the same stanza. The class is reading a:

a. Sonnet
b. Villanelle
c. Sestina
d. Limerick

49. Among the following, which is NOT a common academic standard for kindergarten students in decoding and identifying words?

a. Showing knowledge that letter sequences correspond to phoneme sequences
b. Understanding that word sounds and meanings change along with word letters
c. Decoding monosyllabic words using initial and final consonant and vowel sounds
d. Matching letters to consonant sounds; reading simple, monosyllabic sight words

50. Which of the following is true of the introduction to a written piece?

a. It is best to write it first.
b. It is best to write it last.
c. It should reinforce the points made in the piece.
d. It is the least important part of a piece of writing.

Mathematics

1. In a class of 24 students, 18 completed their projects on time. What fraction of the students failed to complete their projects on time?

a. 1/4
b. 2/3
c. 3/4
d. 5/8

2. The factors $(x-3)$, $(x-4)$ and $(x+7)$ expand to give the equation:

a. $x^3 - 12x^2 - 7x + 84$
b. $x^3 + 84x^2 - 14x + 14$
c. $x^3 - 37x + 84$
d. $x^3 + 14x^2 - 7x + 84$

3. When multiplied together the two complex numbers $(6+5i)$ and $(3-3i)$ yield:

a. $(18-15i)$
b. $(33-3i)$
c. $(33-9i)$
d. $(33-15i)$

4. Given that the value of x is between 0 and 5, but not equal to either 0 or 5, which statement is true?

a. $0 \leq x^2 \leq 5$
b. $0 < x^2 < 25$
c. $0 \leq x^2 \leq 25$
d. $x^2 \leq 25$

5. If $2^n = 6$ and $2^8 = 256$, then $2^8 \times 2^n =$

a. 262
b. 2^{n+8}
c. 2^{8n}
d. $2^n + 6$

6. The series sum of $\frac{1}{n}$ for integer values of n such that $1 \leq n \leq 6$ is:

a. $2\frac{1}{2}$
b. $2\frac{9}{20}$
c. $2\frac{5}{6}$
d. $2\frac{3}{20}$

7. The series sum of $\left(n + \frac{1}{n}\right)$ for integer values $1 \leq n \leq 4$ is:

a. 11
b. A rational real number
c. A complex number
d. An integer

8. Tomas held out both hands, clearly showing ten digits – eight fingers and two thumbs – and proclaimed "I actually have nine fingers!" His friend Jerzy replied "No, you only have eight fingers!". To prove that he had nine fingers Tomas counted backward on one hand "$8 - 7 - 6 - 5$", then said "and 4 on this hand makes 9 fingers". This logic is incorrect because:

a. Tomas counted his thumb as one of the fingers
b. Tomas was mixing ordinal and cardinal numbers
c. Tomas began counting from the left instead of the right
d. Tomas began counting from the right instead of the left

9. The sum of two prime numbers is:

a. Always odd
b. Always a prime number
c. Always even
d. None of the above

10. $(x - 6)$ is a factor of the equation $2x^3 + 4x^2 - 82x - 84 = 0$. If the $(x - 6)$ factor is divided out, the remainder has:

a. Negative integral roots
b. Negative complex roots
c. Negative irrational roots
d. Both positive and negative roots

11. The necessary and sufficient condition for a prime number is:

a. Divisible only by itself and 1
b. Divisible only by itself
c. Is not a product of two numbers
d. Is the product of prime numbers

12. The ratio of 10 to 17.5 is:

a. 1.75
b. Real, rational
c. $\frac{2}{3.5}$
d. Both b and c

13. Which of the following equations may be used to convert $0.\overline{4}$ to a fraction?

a. $10x - x = 4.\overline{4} - 0.\overline{4}$
b. $100x - x = 4.\overline{4} - 0.\overline{4}$
c. $10x - x = 44.\overline{4} - 4.\overline{4}$
d. $100x - 10x = 4.\overline{4} - 0.\overline{4}$

14. Which expression is represented by the diagram below?

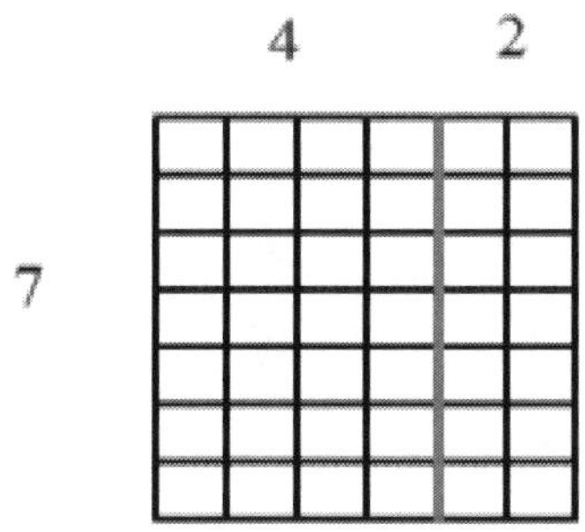

a. $7 + (4 + 2)$
b. $7 \times (4 \times 2)$
c. $7 + (4 \times 2)$
d. $7 \times (4 + 2)$

15. The function $f(x) = \frac{2x^2}{3} + 2x + 3$ has intercepts at:

a. (0,3) and (2,0)
b. (0,3) only
c. (3,0) and (0,3)
d. None of the above

T16. here are three branches in a particular electrical circuit. An indicator light is on (True) if both the first and third branches are active (True) or if the second and third branches are active (True), but not (False) if both the first and second branches are active. The truth table for the indicator light is

a.

1	T	T	T	T	F	F	F	F
2	T	T	T	T	F	F	T	T
3	F	T	F	T	F	T	F	T
Light	F	T	F	F	F	F	F	T

b.

1	T	T	T	T	F	F	T	T
2	F	T	T	T	F	F	F	F
3	F	T	F	T	F	T	F	F
Light	F	T	F	F	T	F	F	F

c.

1	TT	TT	TT	TT	TF	FT	FF	FF
2	FF	FF	TT	TT	FF	FT	TT	TT
3	FF	TT	FF	TT	FF	TT	FF	TT
Light	TT	TT	FF	FF	FF	TF	FF	TT

d.

1	T	T	T	T	F	F	F	F
2	F	F	T	T	F	F	T	T
3	F	T	F	T	F	T	F	T
Light	F	T	F	F	F	F	F	T

17. The graph of the function $y = x^2 - 2x + 6$ has a minimum value at:

a. (1,5)
b. (1,−2)
c. (0,6)
d. (1,6)

18. The equation $x^2 - 2x + 3$ has roots:

a. $-2,\ 3$
b. $1 + i\sqrt{2}, 1 - i\sqrt{2}$
c. $2 + i\sqrt{3}, 2 - i\sqrt{3}$
d. $6 - i\sqrt{2}, 6 + i\sqrt{2}$

19. The value of 7! divided by 3! is:

a. 2.33
b. 840
c. 210
d. 1,320

20. The graph of $x^2 + y^2 = 25$ intersects the line $y = x + 5$ at coordinates:

a. (1,6) and (4,−1)
b. (0,5) and (−5,0)
c. (−4,1) and (0,5)
d. (3,4) and (4,3)

21. An equation of a hyperbola has the form:

a. $y = ax$
b. $y = ax^2 + b$
c. $x^2 - y^2 = a$
d. $x^2 + y^2 = a$

22. Which of the following formulas may be used to represent the sequence 1, 2, 4, 8, 16, ...?

a. $y = 2x$
b. $y = x + 2$
c. $y = 2^{x-1}$
d. $y = x^2$

23. Which of the following represents the graph of $y = (x - 4)^2 + 3$?

a.
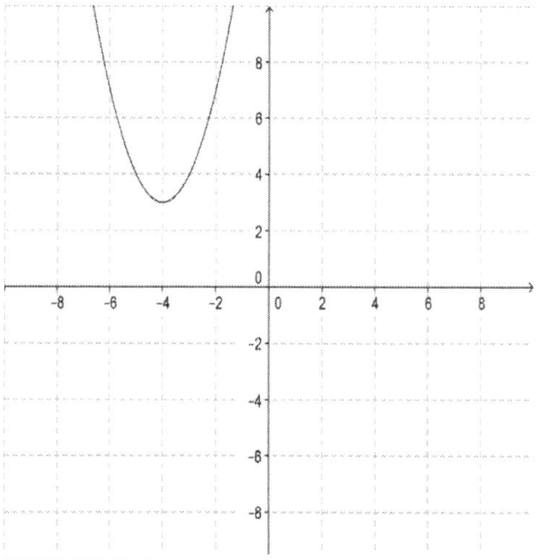

b.
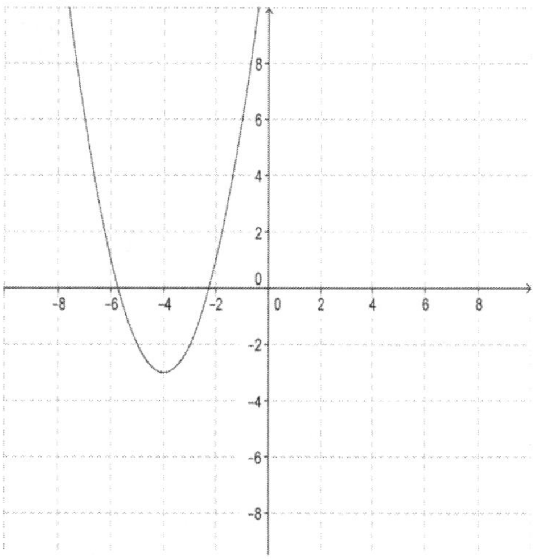

c.
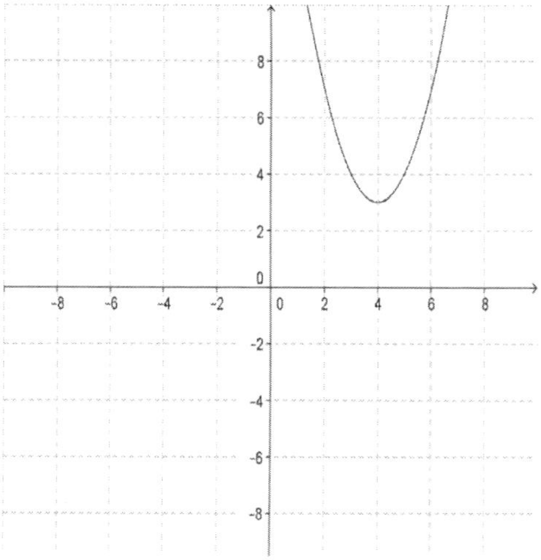

d.
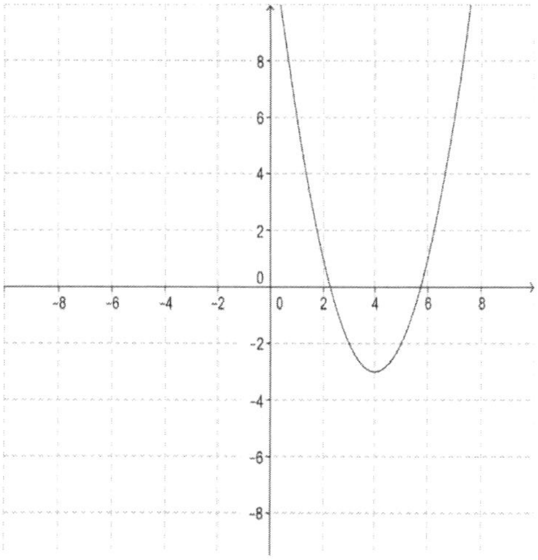

24. Which of the following represents an inversely proportional relationship?

a. $y = 3x$
b. $y = \frac{1}{3}x$
c. $y = \frac{3}{x}$
d. $y = 3x^2$

25. Elijah pays a $30 park entrance fee plus $4 for every ticket purchased. Which of the following equations represents the cost?

a. $y = 30x + 4$
b. $y = 34x$
c. $y = 4x + 30$
d. $y = 34x + 30$

26. A round cylinder has radius r and height h. It has a total surface area of:

a. $\pi r^2 h$
b. $2\pi r(h + r)$
c. $2\pi dh$
d. $2\pi r^2 + h$

27. A triangular prism has a right triangle cross-section. The orthogonal sides are each 2 cm wide, and the total length of the prism is 10 cm. The total surface area of the prism and its volume are:

a. $(44 + 10\sqrt{2})$ cm^2 and 20 cm^3
b. $64\sqrt{2}$ cm^2 and 20 cm^3
c. 42 cm^2 and 22 cm^3
d. $(44 + 20\sqrt{2})$ cm^2 and 20 cm^3

28. What is the educational purpose of having students measure the length of an object, such as their desk or table, with non-standard measuring units smaller than the object, such as crayons?

a. Measuring with small units is easier for young children
b. Children cannot read the markings on a standard ruler or yard stick
c. Students learn to measure something larger than a unit with repetitive use of that unit
d. Students will later be able to transfer measurements from meters to yards

29. A complex right triangle has orthogonal sides of length $(6 + 3i)$ and $(4 + i\sqrt{3})$. The hypotenuse has the length:

a. $\sqrt{40 + 4i(9 + 2\sqrt{3})}$
b. $\sqrt{40 + i(36 + 2\sqrt{3})}$
c. $40 + 4i(9 + 2\sqrt{3})$
d. $40 + i(36 + 2\sqrt{3})$

30. A large L-shaped field is 400 m long on its longest side, and 150 m wide at its widest point. The opposite parallel sides are only $\frac{1}{5}$ as long. The total perimeter of the field is:

a. 6,000 m
b. 900 m
c. 1,200 m
d. 1,100 m

31. The total perimeter of an L-shaped field is 800 feet. The longest side is 300 feet, and the longest width is 100 feet. The shorter sides are 50 feet and 50 feet respectively. The total area of the field is:

a. 22,500 square feet
b. 30,000 square feet
c. 17,500 square feet
d. 45,000 square feet

32. A city is at an elevation of 6,700 feet. Which of the following best represents the elevation in miles?

a. 0.77 miles
b. 1.27 miles
c. 1.56 miles
d. 1.89 miles

33. A can has a radius of 1.5 inches and a height of 3 inches. Which of the following best represents the volume of the can?

a. 17.2 in^3
b. 19.4 in^3
c. 21.2 in^3
d. 23.4 in^3

34. A magician has a hat that holds two rabbits. One rabbit is black and the other is white. In his last 16 performances he has randomly pulled the black rabbit from the hat 16 times. The probability that he will pull the white rabbit from the hat in his next performance is:

a. 0.50
b. 1
c. $\frac{1}{17}$
d. 0

35. A bag contains 16 coins, each with a different date. The number of possible combinations of three coins from the bag is:

a. 650
b. 48
c. 560
d. 6

36. Ten sample values were found to be 6, 7, 7, 9, 5, 7, 8, 2, 6 and 3. The mean and median values of these samples are:

a. 6 and 6.5
b. 6 and 7
c. 6 and 8
d. 6.5 and 7

37. Seven samples were obtained having the values 21, 22, 26, 29, 27, 26 and 24. The mean and standard deviation values are:

a. 22.4 and 2.6
b. 25 and 2.2
c. 25 and 2.6
d. 25.6 and 2.2

38. A certain special die has eight sides instead of six. The probability of rolling an odd number is:

a. The same as for a six-sided die
b. One-third more than for a six-sided die
c. One-third less than for a six-sided die
d. 25% greater

39. Kayla rolls a die and tosses a coin. What is the probability she gets an even number and heads?

a. $\frac{1}{6}$
b. $\frac{1}{4}$
c. $\frac{1}{3}$
d. 1

40. How many ways can 1st – 3rd place winners be chosen from 6 people?

a. 120
b. 60
c. 30
d. 20

41. What is the limit of the series below?

$$1+\frac{1}{2}+\frac{1}{4}+\frac{1}{8}+\frac{1}{16}+\cdots$$

a. 2
b. $2\frac{1}{4}$
c. $2\frac{3}{4}$
d. 3

42. 320 students are surveyed. 120 of the students like only Dallas. 150 of the students like only Houston. 48 of the students like neither city. How many students like Dallas *and* Houston?

a. 2
b. 3
c. 4
d. 5

43. A man standing on a flat, level surface casts a shadow that is 6.2 ft in length. The man is 5.8 ft tall. Which of the following best represents the distance from the top of his head to the end of the shadow?

a. 7 ft
b. 7.5 ft
c. 8 ft
d. 8.5 ft

44. If the midpoint of a line segment graphed on the xy-coordinate plane is $(3,-1)$ and the slope of the line segment is -2, which of these is a possible endpoint of the line segment?

a. $(-1,1)$
b. $(0,-5)$
c. $(7,1)$
d. $(5,-5)$

45. Which of the following statements is NOT true?

a. In a skewed distribution, the mean is pulled towards the tail.
b. In a skewed distribution, the mean is pulled towards the area with a higher frequency of scores.
c. In a normal distribution, the mean, median, and mode are the same value.
d. The area under a normal curve is 1.

46. Which of the following is an example of an ordinal number?

a. 13
b. One-half
c. Second
d. Ten

47. Mrs. Miller is teaching a unit on numbers and operations with her sixth-grade class. At the beginning of class, she asks the students to work in groups to sketch a Venn diagram to classify whole numbers, integers, and rational numbers on a white board. Which of the following types of assessments has the teacher used?

a. Summative assessment
b. Formative assessment
c. Formal assessment
d. Informal assessment

48. Which of these is NOT a net of a cube?

a.
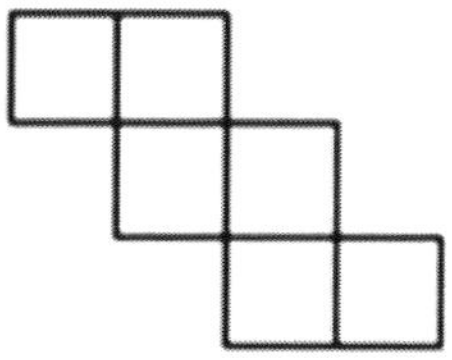
b.
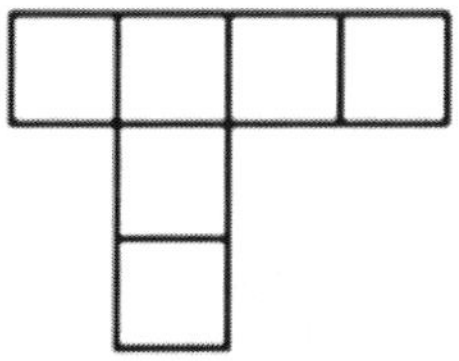
c.
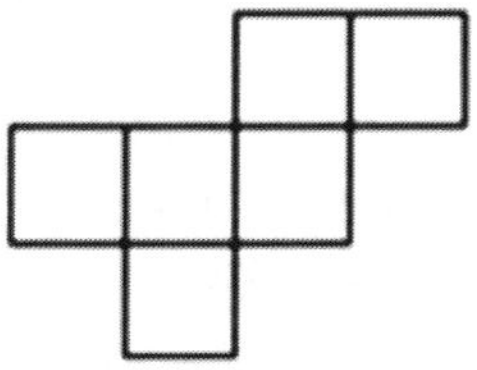
d.
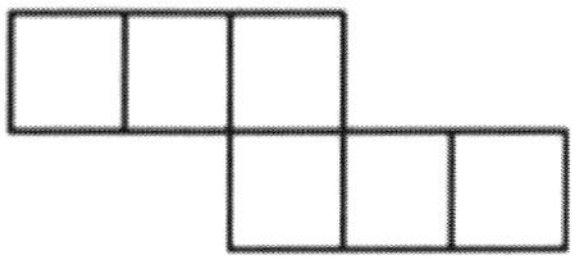

49. Determine the number of diagonals of a dodecagon.

a. 12
b. 24
c. 54
d. 108

50. $A = \{5, 9, 2, 3, -1, 8\}$ **and** $B = \{2, 0, 4, 5, 6, 8\}$**. What is** $A \cap B$**?**

a. $\{5, 2, 8\}$
b. $\{-1, 0, 2, 3, 4, 5, 6, 8, 9\}$
c. $\emptyset$
d. $\{5, 8\}$

Science

1. If an astronomer observing the stars detects a blue shift, what could he conclude?

a. The star is moving farther away from him.
b. The star is moving closer or toward him.
c. The star is cooling down and becoming smaller.
d. The star is heating up and becoming larger.

2. Salts are made from a combination of what two types of substances?

a. A metal and a nonmetal
b. A nonmetal and an alkaline earth metal
c. A cation from a base and an anion from an acid
d. A metal and a halogen

3. What group of the periodic table makes up the alkaline earth metals?

a. Group 1
b. Group 2
c. Group 13
d. Group 17

4. Which of the following terms describes an intrusion of magma injected between two layers of sedimentary rock, forcing the overlying strata upward to create a dome-like form?

a. Sill
b. Dike
c. Laccolith
d. Caldera

5. Which of the following statements concerning earthquakes is NOT true?

a. The epicenter is located on the earth's surface directly above the focus.
b. Large earthquakes near or beneath a large body of water can generate deadly tsunamis.
c. The epicenter may be located by combining seismograms from two widely separate locations.
d. P waves, which travel faster than S waves, tend to have lower amplitude than S waves, causing little damage.

6. Which of the following apparent colors of stars indicates the coolest temperature?

a. Orange red
b. Yellow orange
c. Yellow white
d. Blue white

7. Which of the following is NOT a factor as to why lakes don't freeze solid in winter?

a. Water has its lowest volume at zero degrees Celsius.
b. As water freezes, the ice floats due to its lower density than the surrounding water.
c. Due to hydrogen bonding, ice forms six-sided crystals that have a larger volume than six water molecules.
d. The water exposed to the cold air freezes first, forming a good insulator between the air and the water beneath it.

8. Which of the following is a type of physical weathering?

a. Oxidation
b. Hydrolysis
c. Exfoliation
d. Carbonation

9. Which of the following correctly describes cloud formation?

a. Clouds form when evaporation and condensation are in dynamic equilibrium.
b. Clouds form when there are no condensation nuclei in the air.
c. Clouds form when the atmospheric temperature reaches the dew point.
d. Clouds form when the relative humidity is 0%.

10. Which of the following describes the difference between an anabolism reaction and a catabolism reaction?

a. Anabolism undergoes ionic reactions, while catabolism undergoes covalent reactions.
b. Anabolism undergoes condensation reactions, while catabolism undergoes hydrolysis.
c. Anabolism reactions use water, while catabolism reactions do not.
d. Anabolism reactions release glucose, while catabolism reactions release water.

11. Plant A undergoes C4 photosynthesis. What type of environment would the plant most likely live in?

a. Plant A lives in a very moist environment.
b. Plant A lives in a very arid environment.
c. Plant A lives in a marine environment.
d. Plant A lives in a dark environment that lacks solar energy.

12. The following is the anticodon sequence formed during translation. What is the mRNA codon sequence?

A C G U A C G C U

a. T G C A T G C G A
b. U G C T U G C G T
c. U G C A U G C G A
d. U C G A U C G C A

13. A dihybrid cross is made between the dominant genes for brown eyes (B) and blonde hair (S), and the recessive genes for blue eyes (b) and red hair (s). What fraction of offspring would have the genotype BbSs in the F2 generation?

a. $\frac{1}{16}$
b. $\frac{3}{16}$
c. $\frac{4}{16}$
d. $\frac{9}{16}$

14. What type of mutation is represented by the following sequence?

Original: 1 2 3 4 5 6
Mutated: 1 5 4 3 2 6

a. Breakage
b. Deletion
c. Insertion
d. Inversion

15. Which of the following molecules is thought to have acted as the first enzyme in early life on earth?

a. Protein
b. RNA
c. DNA
d. Triglycerides

16. When an animal takes in more energy than it uses over an extended time, the extra chemical energy is stored as:

a. Fat
b. Starch
c. Protein
d. Enzymes

17. A length of DNA coding for a particular protein is called a(n)

a. Allele
b. Genome
c. Gene
d. Transcript

18. Which of the following plant organelles contain pigments that give leaves their color?

a. Centrioles
b. Cell walls
c. Chloroplasts
d. Central vacuole

19. The volume of water in a bucket is 2.5 liters. When an object with an irregular shape and a mass of 40 grams is fully submerged in the water, the total volume becomes 4.5 liters. What is the density of the object?

a. 0.1 g/L
b. 2 g/L
c. 20 g/L
d. 80 g/L

20. Elements on the periodic table are arranged into groups and periods and ordered according to all of the following EXCEPT:

a. Atomic number
b. Refractive index
c. Reactivity
d. Number of protons

21. Which of the following statements about heat transfer is NOT true?

a. As the energy of a system changes, its thermal energy must change or work must be done.
b. Heat transfer from a warmer object to a cooler object can occur spontaneously.
c. Heat transfer can never occur from a cooler object to a warmer object.
d. If two objects reach the same temperature, energy is no longer available for work.

22. Which of the following demonstrations best illustrates Newton's first law?

a. Giving a small push to a billiard ball that was at rest on a smooth, level table and letting it roll on the table
b. Dragging a box on a table at a constant speed by exerting just enough force to overcome the force of friction
c. Trying without success to move a heavy bureau or filing cabinet on the floor
d. Running a current through two parallel wires

23. Which of the following is NOT generally true regarding solubility?

a. Increasing temperature increases the solubility of a solid in a liquid.
b. Increasing temperature increases the solubility of a gas in a liquid.
c. Increasing the pressure has little effect on the solubility of a solid in a liquid.
d. Increasing partial pressure of a gas decreases the solubility of a gas in a liquid.

24. Which of the following is the best description of pressure?

a. Mass per unit volume
b. Force per unit area
c. Force per unit volume
d. Mass per unit area

25. Which of the following characteristics is consistent with an acid?

a. Turns litmus paper blue
b. Accepts a proton
c. Reacts with zinc to produce hydrogen gas
d. Produces OH^- ions in aqueous solutions

26. Which of the following is a solute?

a. Salt in a mixture of salt and pepper
b. Air in a mixture of ash and air
c. Water in a mixture of salt and water
d. Sugar in a mixture of sugar and water

27. Which of the following statements is NOT true about the period of a simple pendulum?

a. As the mass of a pendulum increases, the period increases.
b. For small amplitudes, the period of a pendulum is approximately independent of amplitude.
c. A pendulum swings more slowly at higher elevation.
d. To double the period of a pendulum, the length must be quadrupled.

28. Which of the following is an example of a chemical change?

a. Salt dissolving in water
b. Water evaporating
c. Silver tarnishing
d. Dry ice sublimating

29. Why would it be ethical for local and state governments to conduct a risk-benefit analysis in making decisions about city planning and development?

a. Governments must know what the benefits of a new development are for people and the economy in order to persuade opponents and the public who are against it.
b. Knowledge of the environmental risks and benefits to humans is required for gaining building permits.
c. The benefits to people and the economy must outweigh the risks to determine whether their decision to build is fair.
d. The benefits to people and the economy can be used to ignore the risks associated with any new development.

30. Which of the following ethical questions regarding biotechnology would be answered and regulated by the Food and Drug Administration?

a. Should the packaging of meat products that come from cloned animals be labeled?
b. Should nitrate or sulfate fertilizers be added to oil spills to assist the decomposition of crude oil by bacteria?
c. Should parents be allowed to genetically alter an embryo by choosing its physical characteristics?
d. Should cells or components of cells be used to create industrially useful products?

31. Which of the following is a source of nonrenewable energy?

a. Solar power
b. Wind power
c. Wood
d. Coal

32. All of the following are true regarding wind energy, EXCEPT:

a. Wind turbines use space inefficiently, but they have low operational costs.
b. Wind is not a reliable source of energy in all geographic locations.
c. Wind turbines are expensive to manufacture and install.
d. Wind turbines are a threat to wildlife.

33. A student is working on a science project and is going through each step of the scientific method. After the student conducts his or her first experiment and records the results of the experimental test, what should the student do next?

a. Communicate the results.
b. Draw a conclusion.
c. Repeat the experiment.
d. Create a hypothesis.

34. Once a hypothesis has been verified and accepted, it becomes which of the following?

a. A fact
b. A law
c. A conclusion
d. A theory

35. Which of the following is NOT true concerning forming and testing hypotheses?

a. A controlled experiment should have only one independent variable.
b. A controlled experiment may have several constants.
c. A good hypothesis should take all of the available background material on the topic into consideration.
d. A good hypothesis will not be disproved by testing.

36. Which of the following subskills best fits the process skill of observing?

a. Using the five senses to collect evidence and write descriptions
b. Grouping objects based on similarities, differences, and interrelationships
c. Explaining or interpreting collected evidence
d. Reporting to others what has been found by experimentation

37. Which organisms depend most on light to survive?

a. Undersea plants
b. Mammalians
c. Land plants
d. Humans

38. Which type of rock typically forms on the surface of the earth in cumulative layers?

a. Igneous
b. Obsidian
c. Metamorphic
d. Sedimentary

39. Newton's First law of motion states that:

a. An object at rest tends to stay at rest unless an opposing force changes this.
b. An object stays at rest or in motion unless/until an opposing force changes it.
c. An object in motion tends to stay in motion until an opposing force changes it.
d. For every action that take place, there is an equal and opposite reaction to it.

40. A gas is held in a closed container and held at constant temperature. What is the effect of increasing the volume of the container by 3 times?

a. The pressure is tripled.
b. The pressure increases by one-third.
c. The pressure decreases to one-third.
d. The pressure remains constant.

41. Who was the father of microscopy?

a. Pasteur
b. Koch
c. Leeuwenhoek
d. Watson

42. Students are planning to assemble and operate a small gasoline engine. Which safety concern should have the highest priority?

a. An open fuel tank could release sickening fumes.
b. Fingers could be injured if caught in the gears.
c. Spilled liquids may cause a short in the starter.
d. The exhaust fumes require adequate ventilation.

43. If an atom has a neutral charge, what must be true of the atom?

a. The nucleus contains only neutrons and no protons.
b. The atomic mass is equal to the number of neutrons.
c. The atomic number is equal to the number of neutrons.
d. The atomic number is equal to the number of electrons.

44. Which of the following have a simple life cycle, without a metamorphosis?

a. Frogs
b. Newts
c. Grasshoppers
d. Human beings

45. Which of the following is needed for an experiment to be considered successful?

a. A reasonable hypothesis
b. A well-written lab report
c. Data that others can reproduce
d. Computer-aided statistical analysis

46. What is the scientific definition of work?

a. The amount of energy used to accomplish a job
b. The force used to move a mass over a distance
c. The amount of energy used per unit of time
d. Energy stored in an object due to its position

47. What is a practical purpose for the glass walls of skyscrapers?

a. Decoration
b. Insulation
c. Privacy
d. Support

48. When we look at a straw in a glass of water, the straw appears broken or bent at the waterline. This appearance is a function of:

a. Scattering
b. Absorption
c. Reflection
d. Refraction

49. The stream of charged particles that escape the Sun's gravitational pull is best described by which of the following terms?

a. Solar wind
b. Solar flare
c. Solar radiation
d. Sunspots

50. According to Ohm's Law, how are voltage and current related in an electrical circuit?

a. Voltage and current are inversely proportional to one another.
b. Voltage and current are directly proportional to one another.
c. Voltage acts to oppose the current along an electrical circuit.
d. Voltage acts to decrease the current along an electrical circuit.

Social Studies

1. How did Egypt's geographical features most contribute to the stability of ancient Egyptian culture?

a. The Nile River regularly and predictably flooded, irrigating crops.
b. The expanse of the Nile River prevented Egyptians from settling elsewhere.
c. The Valley of the Kings divided Upper Egypt from Lower Egypt.
d. The Mediterranean Sea enabled contact between Egyptians and other ancient peoples.

2. How does the prevalence of ziggurats in ancient Mesopotamia illustrate a central factor of Mesopotamian culture?

a. Intended as lookouts, the number of ziggurats illustrates a Mesopotamian concern for security from invaders.
b. Used for stargazing, the number of ziggurats shows how Mesopotamian culture depended on astrology.
c. Dedicated to Mesopotamian rulers, the ziggurats illustrate the complete control Mesopotamian kings held over their subjects.
d. Structures dedicated to gods, the ziggurats illustrate the importance of religion in Mesopotamian culture.

3. How did Charlemagne's coronation as Holy Roman Emperor influence European politics?

a. It united much of Western Europe under a single ruler.
b. It strengthened papal authority regarding the right of political leaders to rule.
c. It made Catholicism the official religion throughout Charlemagne's empire.
d. It led to Charlemagne's renunciation of conquest by force.

4. Which statement best describes the feudal society of Western Europe in the Middle Ages?

a. Religious institutions owned most of the land and leased portions to vassals.
b. Rulers granted land strictly on the basis of blood relationships.
c. Rulers granted vassals land in exchange for military and political service.
d. Feudalism shifted a spice-based economy to a land-based economy.

5. What effect did the Crusades have on Europe's Jewish population?

a. Entire European Jewish communities were killed during the First Crusade.
b. Persecution of Jewish people declined as the Crusaders focused on Muslims.
c. Most Jewish traders and merchants profited through Crusades-related business.
d. To avoid persecution, some Jewish-only battalions fought in each Crusade.

6. During the 15th century, Johann Gutenberg invented a printing press with moveable type. How did his invention influence science?

a. It did not influence science; the printing of Gutenberg Bibles directed public attention away from science and toward reforming the Catholic Church.
b. It led to scientific advances throughout Europe by spreading scientific knowledge.
c. It influenced scientific advancement in Germany only, where Gutenberg's press was based.
d. It did not influence science; though texts with scientific knowledge were printed, distribution of these texts was limited.

7. In about 1428, the Mesoamerican city-states Tenochtitlan, Texcoco, and Tlacopan formed a Triple Alliance. How did this influence Aztec history?

a. Texcoco and Tlacopan secretly conspired against Tenochtitlan, using the Alliance as a front.
b. Disagreements about strategy between the city-states weakened Aztec resistance to Spanish invaders.
c. The alliance agreed that each city-state would offer a specific number of human sacrifices each year.
d. The allied city-states joined forces to conquer other city-states, incorporating them into an Aztec Empire.

8. Which statement best describes the role of the Catholic Church in medieval Western Europe?

a. Powerful and wealthy, the Church was important to both poor and rich people.
b. The Church concerned itself mainly with the poorer members of medieval society.
c. Weakened by infighting about Church doctrine, the Church struggled to wield power.
d. The Catholic Church served as a neutral force between competing political leaders.

9. In the 16th century, Akbar ruled the Mughal Empire, which covered much of present-day India. Which statement best describes one means by which Akbar maintained control of the Empire?

a. He paid administrative officials with land instead of money.
b. He accommodated the religious practices of Hindus as well as Muslims.
c. He refused to allow certain defeated rulers to keep their land.
d. He refused to allow the construction of Hindu temples.

10. Which statement best describes the role played by the French economy in causing the 1789 French Revolution?

a. France's very large national debt led to heavy tax burdens on the French peasantry.
b. Nearly sixty percent of annual national expenditures financed luxuries for the French nobility.
c. Reforms in the guild system allowed many peasants to rise to the middle class.
d. The king's attempt to curtail free trade led skilled journeymen to rebel against the monarchy.

11. The Indus Valley or Harappan civilization existed in all of the following modern countries EXCEPT:

a. Iran
b. India
c. Pakistan
d. Turkey

12. The Yellow River Valley began to emerge as a cultural center during the:

a. Shang Dynasty
b. Neolithic Era
c. Xia Dynasty
d. Paleolithic Era

13. Thai food has become increasingly popular in the United States, though it is prepared in slightly different ways here. This is an example of:

a. Cultural divergence
b. Assimilation
c. Cultural convergence
d. Acculturation

14. Which type of chart is best at representing the cycle of demographic transition?

a. Pie chart
b. Political map
c. Line graph
d. Flow-line map

15. Where was the first great human civilization located?

a. Egypt
b. Greece
c. Mesopotamia
d. Samaria

16. Which of the following was NOT an ancient Egyptian ruler?

a. Anubis
b. Hatshepsut
c. Ramses II
d. Tutankhamen

17. How did the Crusader army that went on the First Crusade differ from the Crusader armies that Pope Urban II envisioned?

a. There was no difference. The people of Europe were accustomed to obeying clerical direction and eagerly joined the cause creating an army that was primarily made up of faithful Christians from all social classes led by a select group of knights who were responsible for leading and training their armies.
b. There was no difference. The people of Europe obeyed clerical direction and stayed home to pray for the success of an army composed entirely of knights and other professional military personnel.
c. Pope Urban II had envisioned an army of skilled knights and professional soldiers; instead, men and women from all classes joined together to retake the Holy Land.
d. Pope Urban II had envisioned an army composed of faithful Christians from all social classes led by a group of select knights; instead, the army was primarily made up of knights and other professional military personnel.

18. Which of the following statements is NOT true of daily life for the average European in the 1500s?

a. Life was not significantly different from the medieval era.
b. The majority of people worked in agriculture.
c. Life expectancy was short.
d. Most people were literate, due to well-financed public education programs.

19. Which of these is true concerning the French Revolution, America, and Europe?

a. When France's revolution spread and they went to war with other European countries, George Washington allied with the French.
b. During the time period around 1792, American merchants were trading with countries on both sides of the war.
c. American traders conducted business with various countries, profiting the most from the British West Indies.
d. The Spanish navy retaliated against America for trading with the French by capturing American trading ships.

20. Which of the following is NOT true about the Italian Renaissance?

a. The Black Death killed one third of the population of Europe.
b. The lower classes benefited from the need for laborers.
c. The middle classes developed from a need for services.
d. The upper class invested in banks.

21. Which of the following was NOT a tax levied on the American colonies by the British government in the 1760s and '70s?

a. The Sugar Act of 1764
b. The Stamp Act of 1765
c. The Lead Act of 1772
d. The Tea Act of 1773

22. To whom was the Declaration of Independence addressed and why?

a. To the British Parliament, because the colonists were opposed to being ruled by a king who had only inherited his throne and only considered the popularly elected Parliament to hold any authority over them
b. To the King of England because the colonists were upset that Parliament was passing laws for them even though they did not have the right to elect members of Parliament to represent their interests
c. To the governors of the rebelling colonies so that they would know that they had 30 days to either announce their support of the Revolution or to return to England
d. To the colonial people as a whole. The Declaration of Independence was intended to outline the wrongs that had been inflicted on them by the British military and inspire them to rise up in protest

23. How did the ruling in *Marbury v. Madison* alter the Supreme Court's power in the federal government?

a. It lessened it. The Supreme Court was concerned about the possibility of judges overturning laws enacted by voters through referendums and took away that power.
b. It increased it. The decision in *Marbury v. Madison* gave the Supreme Court its now traditional right to overturn legislation.
c. It increased it. The decision in *Marbury v. Madison* strengthened the Supreme Court's Constitutional right to overturn legislation.
d. There was no change. *Marbury v. Madison* was a case involving a president who was unwilling to obey laws enacted by his predecessor; there was nothing about the case or decision that would have more than a cursory connection to federal powers of government

24. Which President of the United States changed the date of Thanksgiving from the last Thursday of November to the fourth Thursday of November?

a. George Washington
b. Andrew Jackson
c. Abraham Lincoln
d. Franklin D. Roosevelt

25. Which of the following is considered to be the largest cause of death among Native Americans following the arrival of European colonists in North America?

a. Wounds from wars with the European settlers
b. Wounds from wars with the other Native American tribes
c. European diseases
d. Exposure during the wintry, forced marches on which the European settlers forced them

26. Which group(s) of people were originally responsible for selecting the members of the US Senate?

a. State legislatures
b. State governors
c. State electors
d. State residents, subject to voting eligibility

27. The Erie Canal is 363 miles long and connects which body of water to Lake Erie?

a. The Mississippi River
b. The Hudson River
c. The Susquehanna River
d. The Lehigh River

28. The telephone was a solution to which of the following problems with the telegraph?

a. Telegraph lines were thick and difficult to maintain.
b. Telegraph messages could only be received by people who had specialized equipment.
c. Telegraphs could only relay one message at a time.
d. Telegraphs frequently broke down if subject to extended use.

29. Who was Lewis and Clark's guide?

a. Pocahontas
b. Sacagawea
c. Squanto
d. Wauwatosa

30. What was the purpose of Lyndon Johnson's Great Society?

a. To eliminate poverty and racial injustice in America
b. To erase the last vestiges of the Great Depression from the American economic landscape
c. To encourage economic prosperity through trickledown economics
d. To increase educational standards in the United States

31. The writers of *The Federalist Papers* published under the pen name "Publius." Who were the authors?

a. James Madison, John Jay, and Alexander Hamilton
b. George Washington, Thomas Jefferson, and James Madison
c. Alexander Hamilton, Benjamin Franklin, and Thomas Jefferson
d. Benjamin Franklin, John Jay, and Thomas Jefferson

32. Which of the following is a significant structural similarity between the government of the Iroquois Confederacy and the government of the United States?

a. Many decisions require compromise between two separate entities. In the Iroquois Confederacy, those entities were two different sets of Lords; in the US government, those entities are the House of Representatives and the Senate.
b. A single leader has significant executive powers: in the Iroquois Confederacy, a chief, and in the US government, the president.
c. The level of representation in at least one legislative body depended on population. In the Iroquois Confederacy, the population of tribes partially determined representation, and in the United States, the population of states partially determines representation.
d. A third judicial branch served as a check on the executive power in both the Iroquois Confederacy and the US government.

33. One of the earliest political parties in the United States was the Federalist Party. Its decline is best explained by:

a. A failure to organize state political parties
b. The enmity of wealthy Americans
c. Its opposition to the War of 1812
d. Its advocacy of a strong central government

34. In 1777, the United States Congress adopted the Articles of Confederation. The Articles of Confederation limited the power of the federal government by denying it:

a. The power to borrow money
b. The power to declare war
c. The power to make international treaties
d. The power to raise taxes

35. Which statement describes the authority of most local officials?

a. Members of local government are generally elected by the people, but their authority is granted by the state.
b. Members of local government are given their authority directly from the people.
c. Members of local government have constitutionally-granted authority.
d. Members of local government are elected by the people, but the state Supreme Court determines their authority.

36. The economic theories of John Maynard Keynes are most closely associated with which of the following?

a. The view that deficit spending leads to inflation
b. Advocating government action against monopolies
c. The view that supply creates its own demand
d. Advocating government action to stimulate economic growth

37. An action's opportunity cost is best explained in terms of:

a. The minimum amount a business must borrow for the action
b. The opportunities given up in order to pursue that action
c. The percentage of one's overall budget that the action requires
d. The cost of a long-term action adjusted for inflation

38. Assume a society has a given production possibilities frontier (PPF) representing the production of cheese and butter. Which of the following would cause the PPF to move outward?

a. The invention of a new machine that makes cheese more efficiently
b. An increase in the production of butter
c. An increase in the production of cheese
d. A decrease in the production of cheese and butter

39. What does the data in this table most directly describe?

Inputs	1	2	3	4
Output	20	50	80	100

a. The Law of Diminishing Marginal Returns
b. Law of Increasing Opportunity Cost
c. Law of Demand
d. Consumer surplus

40. Which of the following best defines American GDP?

a. The value, in American dollars, of all goods and services produced within American borders during one calendar year
b. The value, in American dollars, of all goods and services produced by American companies during one calendar year
c. The total value, in American dollars, of all American household incomes during one calendar year
d. The value, in American dollars, of a "market basket" of goods and services in one year divided by the value of the same market basket in a previous year multiplied by 100

41. In social sciences, reification is best understood as:

a. Using qualitative data instead of quantitative data
b. Treating an abstraction as a concrete thing
c. The use of heuristic devices
d. Mistaking subjectivity for objectivity

42. Suppose that every time a cat hears a can opener, it is fed. The cat runs to the kitchen to be fed every time it hears a can opener. In psychology, this kind of association is called:

a. Operant conditioning
b. Habituation
c. Classical conditioning
d. Conformity

43. Of the factors listed below, which one is NOT among Max Weber's independent factors associated with his theory of social stratification?

a. Social class
b. Personal power
c. Social status
d. Race

44. Which of the following questions would most likely be asked by a historian concerned with the philosophy of history?

a. What issues shaped the writing of Plato's Republic?
b. Should history be measured by changes in individual lives or by larger political trends?
c. Why were the religions of Shinto and Buddhism able to merge in Japan?
d. Should historians study modern primitive cultures as a means of learning about past civilizations?

45. Which of the following is NOT necessarily an example of an educator introducing his own bias into the educational process?

a. A teacher only using materials and sources that he knows are reputable and declining to use unverified material in his lessons
b. A textbook author choosing to only use sources that place his favorite US president in a good light and his least favorite US president in a bad light
c. A teacher only using primary sources that he agrees with and ridiculing a student who provides a verifiable primary source that offers a conflicting opinion
d. An administrator only selecting textbooks that were written before a certain date to be included in classroom instruction

46. Power divided between local and central branches of government is a definition of what term?

a. Bicameralism
b. Checks and balances
c. Legislative oversight
d. Federalism

47. In Maslow's theory, which needs are at the base of the pyramid?

a. Self-actualizing
b. Physiological
c. Security
d. Esteem

48. As a form of government, what does oligarchy mean?

a. Rule by one
b. Rule by a few
c. Rule by law
d. Rule by many

49. The idea that the purpose of the American colonies was to provide Great Britain with raw materials and a market for its goods is an expression of:

a. Free trade
b. Most favored nation status
c. Mercantilism
d. Laissez-faire capitalism

50. A filibuster is used to delay a bill. Where can a filibuster take place?

a. The House of Representatives
b. The Senate
c. Committees
d. The Supreme Court

Answer Key and Explanations

Reading/Language Arts

1. A: Homophones. Homophones are a type of homonym that sound alike but are spelled differently and have different meanings. Other examples are *two, to*, and *too* and *their, they're*, and *there.*

2. A: A syllable is a minimal sound unit arranged around a vowel. For example, *academic* has four syllables: *a/ca/dem/ic.* It is possible for a syllable to be a single vowel, as in the above example. It is not possible for a syllable to be a single consonant.

3. A: Audience members are most likely to retain the points of a speech or lecture if they are offered in the form of a story and the speaker uses language that is simple and direct enough to be transparent. The stories need to be simple, and must drive the speech directly toward an essential and clear point. Including anecdotes is most effective when the speaker uses storytelling techniques that will bring them alive, such as varying pace, pitch, and intensity, using body language to suggest a change in speakers, and using the stage to suggest a setting.

4. B: A reading teacher offers corrective feedback to a student in order to explain why a particular error in reading is, in fact, an error. Corrective feedback is specific; it locates where and how the student went astray so that similar errors can be avoided in future reading.

5. B: In a cloze test, a reader is given a text with certain words blocked out. The reader must be able to determine probable missing words based on contextual clues. In order to supply these words, the reader must already know them.

6. A: Homophones. Homophones sound alike but are spelled differently and have different meanings. Synonyms share meaning, homographs share the same spelling, and homonyms are like homophones, that share the same sounds, but they also are spelled the same. An example of a homonym is "lie," which can refer to lying down or to untruth.

7. B: Strategizing in order to understand the meaning of a word, knowing multiple meanings of a single word, and applying background knowledge to glean a word's meaning are all ways in which an effective reader enhances vocabulary. Other skills include an awareness of word parts and word origins, the ability to apply word meanings in a variety of content areas, and a delight in learning the meanings of unfamiliar words.

8. D: Suffixes appear at the end of words. Prefixes are attached to the beginning of words to change their meanings. *Un+happy, bi+monthly,* and *re+examine* are prefixes that, by definition, change the meanings of the words to which they are attached.

9. D: A word wall uses visual illustrations of vocabulary words and the concepts they represent, and includes additional words, concepts, and pictures related to the main words and pictures to enrich vocabulary and relational thinking. The teacher would be most responsible for creating the word wall, using it in lessons/activities, and instructing/assisting young children in its use. The children themselves can and will repeatedly sing the same familiar song (A) and repeat the same rhymes and chants (B), which enhance vocabulary development for both native English-speaking and ESL students. Stories (C) may be read live by teachers, or readings may be recorded. Either way, the children play the same role of listening to repeated readings.

10. A: is correct because oral language development begins during infancy and develops until a child has an extensive vocabulary.

11. C: Explaining scientific terms to the student as concepts are presented and related experiments are performed is the most effective strategy because it relates concepts to experiments. The student will not only hear and read the definitions of scientific terms, he will also see them in action, and take part in them. This is likely to be far more effective than the other methods.

12. C: A synonym is a word that has a similar meaning. An antonym is a word that means the opposite. A homonym is a word that sounds the same but has different spelling and meaning. A euphemism is an inoffensive word used in place of an offensive word.

13. B: In cases of words that sound alike but have different meanings, checking a dictionary or thesaurus will ensure correct usage of a word.

14. A: Prefixes appear at the beginning of words, while suffixes appear at the end of words.

15. B: Suffixes appear at the end of words, while prefixes appear at the beginning of words.

16. C: Gregarious means easy to get along with, or friendly. If one didn't know the meaning of the word, the fact that Mary has many friends would be a clue to decipher the meaning.

17. C: Circum is Latin for "around." Post is the prefix for "after." Pre is the prefix for "before." There are several prefixes for "beyond", such as trans, hyper, extra.

18. D: *Poly-* means "many." Although the first thing many people might think of when it comes to this prefix is the word *polyester,* a man-made material that's often used in clothing because it's cheaper than natural materials, it does not mean "artificial."

19. A: This headline uses the simple tense. In this case, it's the simple present tense. B uses the infinitive form, while C and D both drop the auxiliary verb in the passive voice.

20. A: The Latin word *sal* meant "salt." According to the famous ancient historian Pliny the Elder, "in Rome, a soldier was paid in salt," as it was a means of preserving food in the days before refrigeration and was thus a very valuable commodity. The Latin term *salarium,* from the root *sal,* originally meant the salt paid to soldiers but eventually became generalized to mean any kind of payment. (The expression "worth your salt" also derives from this origin.) "Salary" may sound similar to "celery", but their roots and meanings are not the same. While salt eventually referred to any kind of payment including money or other kinds, it never originally meant *money.* "Earnings" is a Modern English synonym for "salary" rather than the original meaning of its root word.

21. B: The word *brunch* is a blend of *breakfast* and *lunch.* Blends of two or more words are known as portmanteau words. (*Portmanteau* is a French word meaning a suitcase.) "Fax" (A) is an example of clipping, or shortening a word, from its original "facsimile." "Babysitter" (C) is an example of compounding, or combining two or more words into one. "Saxophone" (D) is an example of proper noun transfer: A Belgian family that built musical instruments had the last name of Sax, and this wind instrument was named after them. These represent some of the ways that new words have entered—and still do enter—the English language.

22. C: Neologisms (from neo- meaning "new"), also known as "creative coinages," are new words invented by people which then become parts of our vocabulary. The word "quark" was first coined by the great Irish author James Joyce; he used it in his last novel, *Finnegans Wake.* The physicist

Murray Gell-Mann then chose this word from Joyce's work to name the model of elementary particles he proposed (also proposed concurrently and independently by physicist George Zweig) in 1964. Blending (A) is another way new words come into our language; for example, "moped" is a blend of the respective first syllables of "motor" and "pedal." Conversion (B), also called functional shift, changes a word's part of speech. For example, the common nouns "network," "microwave," and "fax," along with the proper noun "Google" have all been converted to verbs in modern usage. Onomatopoeia (D) means words that imitate associated sounds, such as "meow" and "click."

23. C: A euphemism is an expression used instead of more literal words to make a harsh expression sound softer, to make an impolite description sound more polite, or to make a description less polite (such as saying *bit the dust* instead of *died* in a formal setting). Jargon is the specialized terminology of a specific field or group. This example, however, is not medical jargon; a better example might be *expired* or *deceased*. Ambiguity means unclear and/or open to multiple interpretations. A better example of ambiguity in this scenario might be, "The surgery did not obtain all of the desired outcomes." This can mean a greater number of things than that the patient died. A connotation is a suggested meaning associated with the literal meaning of a word. For example, "The surgery was abortive" does not state that the patient died, but if the surgery was meant to save the patient's life, the adjective *abortive*, meaning unsuccessful or failing to obtain the desired result, could connote that the patient died.

24. D: Oral language development requires teamwork, planning, and cooperation

25. D: For the vast majority of people attending a presentation in a foreign country, English will not be their native language, and many of them will struggle to keep up with a presentation in English, so it should not be complex, or very long. It would be wise to include, not avoid, anecdotes from the country, and quotes from nationals. American idioms should be avoided, as idioms by their nature do not translate well.

26. C: Ross told Janine that the secret message is inserted into a bigger message, but isn't seen by anyone who isn't looking for it because it's so small. It's effectively hidden.

27. D: President Lincoln's Gettysburg Address was about all three of these elements. Its primary purpose was a dedication of lives lost on this battlefield, but it was also about the future of America, and it is now famous as an eloquent expression of democratic ideals.

28. B: Relational messages, as opposed to content messages, are concerned with the relationship between a speaker and a recipient rather than with the overt subject of the communication. They may convey belonging, respect, or disapproval, among other things. They are frequently largely or entirely nonverbal; because of this, they may be supported with verbal feedback to confirm them. The content of the message, "Should I come over after work?" is a logistical request. If a speaker leans forward to touch a recipient who is weeping, the relational message is "Do you need my support?" The recipient might respond with a nod and a grateful look, or might clarify the speaker's offer by saying, "I won't be good company, but you can come."

29. B: A strong argument is not made by forcing people to pay attention, interrupting another speaker, or belittling an idea, person, or group. These behaviors simply weaken the speaker's position because they each demonstrate in a different way that the speaker is not in control of his own ideas, and must therefore try to control the situation by using emotion. The most successful arguments acknowledge the strongest points of the opposition, and then unemotionally dissect those points in order to find and demonstrate how they are flawed.

30. C: Every school child is taught that metaphor is the direct comparison of two different things. An example of a metaphor is: "The clouds are pillows of cotton." Looking more deeply into the heart of how metaphor operates, however, it is clear that it is an effective rhetorical device. Metaphor simultaneously allows for great linguistic economy while inviting listeners to embrace new ideas by linking them to ideas with which they are already comfortable and familiar.

31. E: Theoretically, no message arrives intact. Words ultimately don't mean the same thing to different people, so messages can easily be misinterpreted. A sender assumes recipients will interpret the meaning of each word in the same way, which can result in interpersonal communications being unclear. Gender, culture, and age contribute greatly to how speakers formulate and interpret messages. The message's physical environment can contribute to confusion due to distractions. The relationship the sender and receiver share, as well as the relationships under discussion, all shade a message's meaning.

32. C: Effective eye contact suggests confidence, piques audience interest, makes the speaker's message seem familiar, and suggests the speaker is an expert on her subject. Excessive eye contact, however, can cause considerable discomfort for audience members. Audience members enjoy being singled out briefly and made to feel special. Holding a gaze for too long, however, removes the protective sense of anonymity, and can make someone in the audience feel embarrassed, uncertain, or even angry.

33. C: According to the Association of College and Research Libraries, information literacy is the set of skills that an individual must have for finding, retrieving, analyzing, and using information. It is required not just for reading and understanding information (A). Information literacy does not mean learning and retaining a lot of information (B), or only sharing it with others (D), but rather knowing how to find information one does not already have and how to evaluate that information critically for its quality and apply it judiciously to meet one's purposes.

34. D: There are four main components to an effective outline. Subordination means that the information in the heading is more general, while the subheadings are more specific. For example:

I. Visit and Evaluate College Websites

A. Note important statistic

B. Look for interesting classes

The other three components of an effective outline include parallelism, coordination, and division.

35. A: Prewriting must occur before drafting. Conferencing refers to collaborating with others so they may critique the draft or offer suggestions to improve it. Revising and editing both refer to changes a writer makes to a draft to improve it. Since choices B, C, and D are meant to help a writer improve a draft, they cannot be completed before the first draft is written.

36. B: Word associations require a student to pull from previous knowledge or experience. For example, if the student is presented with the word *aardvark* but has never seen or heard of an aardvark, he or she will not be able to make associations. While word association may be a good activity for students after they have reviewed the vocabulary words, it may be counterproductive if the students are unfamiliar with the words. Teachers should also be mindful of cultural differences that may account for a variation in previous knowledge.

37. B: In the Spanish language, the letter h is typically silent. Because the student is an ELL and the USA has many people—both immigrants and those born here—whose first and/or only language is Spanish, this is the first factor to consider among the choices. An articulation disorder (A) is possible, but the teacher should not assume this first with an ELL student. (An SLP evaluation can determine the difference.) While a hearing assessment (C) is always a good idea, if /h/ omission were due to hearing loss the student would likely omit or distort other unvoiced fricatives like /f/, /s/, /ʃ/, and /θ/. If the student had a breathing problem (D), other symptoms would occur in addition to not articulating /h/.

38. C: *Drip, chirp, splash, giggle*. Onomatopoeia refers to words that sound like what they represent.

39. A: Individuals with dysgraphia have difficulty with the physical act of writing. They find holding and manipulating a pencil problematic. Their letters are primitively formed, and their handwriting is illegible.

40. A: Action and adventure stories do not rely on magical or supernatural events as do fantasy, horror, and ghost stories. They are not biographical unless telling the life of a real person.

41. A: Prefixes and suffixes are important for reading comprehension because they change the meanings of the root word to which they are attached. A student who understands that *un* means "not" will be able to decipher the meanings of words such as *unwanted, unhappy,* or *unreasonable.*

42. D: Round-robin reading is a common practice in language arts classes and has been for many years. In this process, students take turns reading aloud for their peers. Other students are asked to follow along silently in their texts while a peer is reading. This strategy does provide a way for students to read texts in class and include as many students as possible, which is often the intended outcome. However, this process often creates a boring atmosphere, since only one student at a time is actively engaged. While that student is reading, other students may become distracted by their own thoughts, other school work, or off-task interaction with each other. All of these issues subvert the intended outcome of the process. There is rarely enough time for each student to practice reading aloud to build students' reading fluency or comprehension in significant ways.

43. C: Because this student loves reading graphic novels and has both talent and enjoyment in drawing, having him create his own graphic novels is a good way to motivate him to write by using his visual style, ability, and interest to access writing activity. Giving audio recordings (A) to a highly visual student is not as appropriate to his strengths and interests. Letting him substitute drawing pictures for all writing assignments (B) would address his strengths and interests but not his needs for learning to write. Having him watch animated videos about writing (D) would suit his visual learning style but would not give him the actual writing practice he needs.

44. A: A fallacy of inconsistency exists in a statement that contradicts itself or defeats itself. Saying there are exceptions to all general statements is itself a general statement; therefore, according to the content, this statement must also have an exception, implying there are NOT exceptions to all general statements. Choice B is an example of a fallacy of irrelevance: passing or failing is determined by course performance, so asking to pass because parents will be upset if one fails is an irrelevant reason for appealing to a teacher for a passing grade. Choice C is an example of a fallacy of insufficiency: a statement is made with insufficient evidence to support it. A lack of evidence of innocence is not enough to prove one is guilty because there could also be an equal lack of evidence of guilt. Choice D is an example of a fallacy of inappropriate presumption: asking someone if he or she has stopped cheating presumes that he or she has cheated in the past. The person being asked this question cannot answer either "yes" or "no" without confirming that he or she has indeed been cheating. If the person being asked has not been cheating, then the person asking the question is making a false assumption.

45. A: In choice A, the teacher guides previewing of information to show students how to put themselves in the right frame of mind to listen carefully for meaning. Students are then able to listen in a guided way based upon the previewing. By varying the type of comprehension assessment, the teacher will get a better understanding of what the students learned. Choice B is a good exercise but does not provide for direct instruction by the teacher or a particularly skilled student. In Choice C, students are focusing more on reading comprehension than listening since they must read the story to themselves and then write a report. There is then no way to gauge what they have learned. Choice D would be useful but does not include teacher-guided previewing, which is very helpful in building comprehension.

46. A: Cooperative learning occurs when a group of students at various levels of reading ability have goals in common. Reading comprehension is achieved through reading both orally and silently, developing vocabulary, a reader's ability to predict what will occur in a piece of writing, a reader's ability to summarize the main points in a piece of writing, and a reader's ability to reflect on the text's meaning and connect that meaning to another text or personal experience.

47. B: Analogies are easier for children to understand because they compare known items, whereas metaphors require abstract thinking.

48. A: There are three primary types of sonnets. The Shakespearean sonnet is specifically what these students are reading. A Spenserian sonnet is also composed of three four-line stanzas followed by a two-line couplet; however, the rhymes are not contained within each stanza but spill from one stanza to the next (*abab bcbc cdcd ee).* A Petrarchan sonnet divides into an eight-line stanza and a six-line stanza.

49. C: Decoding monosyllabic words by referring to the initial and final consonant, short vowel, and long vowel sounds represented by their letters is a common academic standard for 1st-grade students. Typical academic standards for kindergarten students include demonstrating knowledge of letter-sound correspondences; understanding the alphabetic principle; matching letters to their corresponding consonant (and short vowel) sounds; and reading simple, monosyllabic sight words, i.e., high-frequency words.

50. B: In most cases, it is best to write the introduction last. Although it is the first part of the finished work, the introduction provides a synopsis for what is in the entire document. Until the writing is complete, the writer cannot reflect on the work as a whole. Writing the introduction prior to the body runs the risk that what follows may not completely conform to the ideas expressed in the introduction. An introduction usually should not reinforce ideas made in the piece, as the body portion of a work is the best place to flesh out ideas. Answer D is incorrect because an introduction frames the rest of the work; it is an incorrect generalization that the introduction, body, or conclusion are always the most or least important parts.

Mathematics

1. A: If 18 of 24 students completed their projects, then 6 of 24 failed to do so. $\frac{6}{24} = \frac{1}{4}$.

2. C: Multiplication of $x - 3$ by $x - 4$ yields the quadratic expression $x^2 - 7x + 12$. When multiplied by the third factor $x + 7$, this produces the expression $x^3 - 37x + 84$.

3. B: Complex numbers are multiplied out in the same manner as algebraic factors. The difference in the calculation is that any i^2 terms are replaced by the factor (-1).

$$(6 + 5i)(3 - 3i) = 18 - 18i + 15i - 15i^2$$

Since $i = \sqrt{-1}$, substitute (-1) for i^2:

$$18 - 3i - 15(-1) = 18 + 15 - 3i = 33 - 3i$$

4. B: Since x is not equal to either 0 or 5, the value of x^2 also cannot be equal to either 0 or 25. The other options fail to exclude both of these values.

5. B: The general rule for the multiplication of indices is $a^x a^y = a^{x+y}$.

6. B: The series expands to $1 + \frac{1}{2} + \frac{1}{3} + \frac{1}{4} + \frac{1}{5} + \frac{1}{6}$. Some of the fractions can be grouped to simplify, $\frac{1}{2} + \frac{1}{3} + \frac{1}{6} = \frac{3}{6} + \frac{2}{6} + \frac{1}{6} = 1$. This leaves only $\frac{1}{4}$ and $\frac{1}{5}$, which can be combined with a common denominator as $\frac{5}{20} + \frac{4}{20} = \frac{9}{20}$. Adding these values yields $1 + 1 + \frac{9}{20} = 2\frac{9}{20}$.

7. B: The series expands to $\left(1 + \frac{1}{1}\right) + \left(2 + \frac{1}{2}\right) + \left(3 + \frac{1}{3}\right) + \left(4 + \frac{1}{4}\right) = 12\frac{1}{12}$. Though not equal to 11, this is a real rational number.

8. B: When mixing ordinal and cardinal numbers the point of reference shifts by one unit. Ordinal numbering begins from 1, while cardinal numbering begins from 0.

9. D: The first three answers are easily disproved. Two, three and five are all prime numbers. The sum of three and five is eight, an even number and not a prime number. The sum of two and three is five, an odd number.

10. A: Factoring out an $x - 6$ term leaves $2x^2 + 16x + 14 = 0$. Using the general formula for finding the roots of a quadratic equation $x = \frac{-b \pm \sqrt{b^2 - 4ac}}{2a}$, substitute the values of a, b, and c (2, 16, and 14) and complete the calculation to obtain the root values $x = -1$ and $x = -7$, which are negative integers.

11. A: A prime number is by definition any number that can be divided integrally only by itself and 1. It therefore has no factors and so is not the product of any other numbers, prime or otherwise.

12. D: The ratio of 17.5 to 10 is 1.75. The ratio of 10 to 17.5 is $\frac{4}{7} = 0.5714285$, a real, rational number that is equivalent to the ratio of $\frac{2}{3.5}$.

13. A: The repeating decimal may be converted to a fraction by writing:

$$\begin{array}{r} 10x = 4.\overline{4} \\ - \quad x = 0.\overline{4} \\ \hline \end{array}$$

which simplifies as $10x - x = 4.\overline{4} - 0.\overline{4}$.

14. D: The rectangular array represents the product of the side lengths of 7 and $(4 + 2)$, resulting in the expression $7 \times (4 + 2)$.

15. B: The y-intercept at $x = 0$ has the value $f(x) = 3$. For an x-intercept, the value of $f(x)$ must be 0 for some real value of x, but $f(x)$ in this case never has a value less than 1.5.

16. D: The first and third or the second and third branches of the circuit are represented as active in the second, fourth and eighth columns. But in the fourth column the first and second branches are indicated as active, negating the 'Light on' signal.

17. A: Since there are only two values for x, plug in each to see what the corresponding y-value would be. Plugging in 1 and 0 yields 5 and 6, respectively. Since 5 is less than 6, the point representing the minimum of the function is (1,5).

18. B: Using the general formula for finding the roots of a quadratic equation: $x = \frac{-b\pm\sqrt{b^2-4ac}}{2a}$, substitute the values of a, b, and c (1, -2, and 3) and complete the calculation.

$$x = \frac{2 \pm \sqrt{4 - 12}}{2} = 1 \pm i\sqrt{2}$$

19. B: Seven factorial is calculated as $7! = 7 \times 6 \times 5 \times 4 \times 3 \times 2 \times 1$. Similarly, three factorial is calculated as $3! = 3 \times 2 \times 1$. The value of $\frac{7!}{3!}$ then is $7 \times 6 \times 5 \times 4 = 840$.

20. B: At the intersection points, the two functions must have identical values. Substituting the value of $y = x + 5$ into the other equation and solving the resulting quadratic equation produces the root values of $x = 0$ and $x = -5$. The corresponding y-coordinate values are determined by substituting these values into the linear equation.

21. C: The first formula describes a straight line that passes through the origin at (0,0), the second describes a parabola with y-intercept at b, and the fourth describes a circle centered on the origin with radius $\sqrt{a}$.

22. C: The ratio between successive terms is constant (2), so this is a geometric series. A geometric sequence is represented by an exponential function.

23. C: This graph is shifted 4 units to the right, because of the $x - 4$, and 3 units up, because of the $+3$, from that of the parent function, $y = x^2$.

24. C: An inversely proportional relationship is written in the form $y = \frac{k}{x}$, thus the equation $y = \frac{3}{x}$ shows that y is inversely proportional to x.

25. C: The slope is equal to 4, since each ticket costs $4. The y-intercept is represented by the constant fee of $30. Substituting 4 for m and 30 for b into the equation $y = mx + b$ gives $y = 4x + 30$.

26. B: The total surface area of the cylinder is the sum of the two circular ends plus the outer surface of the body. The outer surface can be represented as a plane rectangle of which two sides are the height, and the other two sides are the circumference of the base. The circumference is $2\pi r$ and the height is h. The area of each end of the cylinder is the area of the circle πr^2 and there are two ends, so the area of both ends is $2\pi r^2$. The total surface area of the cylinder is therefore $2\pi rh + 2\pi r^2$ or $2\pi r(h + r)$.

27. D: The cross-section of the prism is a right triangle with orthogonal sides of 2 cm. The hypotenuse side is $\sqrt{8} = 2\sqrt{2}$ cm. The perimeter of the triangular base then is $2 + 2 + 2\sqrt{2}$ or

$4 + 2\sqrt{2}$ cm. Multiplying this by the length gives the surface area of the sides, which is $\left(40 + 20\sqrt{2}\right)$. The surface area of the two ends is calculated as $2\left(\frac{1}{2}bh\right)$, which is 4 cm^2. The total surface area of the prism is therefore $\left(44 + 20\sqrt{2}\right)$ cm^2. The volume is calculated by multiplying the area of the base by the height: $\frac{1}{2}bh \times l = 2 \times 10 = 20$ cm^3.

28. C: This exercise is a way to lay the foundation for measuring techniques and spatial awareness.

29. A: Because the complex triangle is a right triangle, the Pythagorean theorem applies.

$$a^2 + b^2 = c^2 = (6 + 3i)^2 + \left(4 + i\sqrt{3}\right)^2 = (36 + 36i + 9i^2) + \left(16 + 8i\sqrt{3} + 3i^2\right)$$

$$c^2 = 36 - 9 + 16 - 3 + 36i + 8i\sqrt{3} = 40 + 4i\left(9 + 2\sqrt{3}\right)$$

$$c = \sqrt{40 + 4i\left(9 + 2\sqrt{3}\right)}$$

30. D: The perimeter is the total length of the outside edge of the field. Because the sides of the field are orthogonal and parallel, the indented sides do not change the length of the boundaries of the field, only their relative positions.

31. C: This may be solved in a few different ways, each of which involves calculating the area of two rectangular sections whose areas can be calculated directly. The area of the L can be split into two pieces, a 300 ft by 50 ft section and a 50 ft by 50 ft section or a 250 ft by 50 ft section and a 100 ft by 50 ft section. In either case, the areas are calculated directly and then summed. The alternative is to view the L as a larger rectangle that has had a smaller rectangle removed from it. In this method, the large rectangle is a 300 ft by 100 ft section, and the smaller rectangle is a 250 ft by 50 ft section. These areas can be calculated and the smaller subtracted from the larger. In both methods, the area comes out to 17,500 ft^2.

32. B: The following proportion may be written and solved for x: $\frac{5{,}280}{1} = \frac{6{,}700}{x}$. Thus, $x \approx 1.27$.

33. C: The volume of a cylinder may be calculated using the formula $V = \pi r^2 h$, where r represents the radius and h represents the height. Substituting 1.5 for r and 3 for h gives $V = \pi(1.5)^2(3)$, which simplifies to $V \approx 21.2$.

34. A: The events, if truly random, are independent of each other. There is therefore an equal probability of pulling the black rabbit or the white rabbit from the hat each time. The probability is therefore 0.50.

35. C: The number of possible combinations of r items from a set of n items can be calculated by the expression $\frac{n!}{(n-r)!r!}$, or in this case, $\frac{16!}{13!\times 3!} = \frac{16\times 15\times 14}{3\times 2\times 1}$. As an alternative to remembering this formula, the problem can be approached logically. If only 1 coin is to be removed there are 16 possibilities. If 2 coins are to be removed, there are 16 possibilities for the first coin, then 15 for the second, but many of these results are repeats. The two coins that are drawn can be arranged two different ways, so the product must be divided by 2. Similarly, if three coins are drawn, there are 16 possibilities for the first coin, 15 for the second, and 14 for the third, but again many of these results are repeats. Three coins can be arranged in six different ways, so this product must be divided by 6. As you can see, this result matches the calculation from the formula above.

36. A: The average is the sum of the values (60) divided by the number of values (10). The median value is the value at which there are equal numbers of greater and lesser values.

37. C: The mean value is calculated as the sum of the values (175) divided by the number of values (7). The standard deviation, s, of the sample set is calculated as the square root of the difference between the average of the actual values squared and the square of the average value.

38. A: A six-sided die has an equal number of odd and even numbers on the six faces. The probability that an odd number will appear when the die is rolled is equal to the probability that an even number will appear, or 0.5. The eight-sided die also has an equal number of odd and even numbers on its eight faces. The probability that an odd number will appear when the die is rolled is therefore also equal to the probability that an even umber will appear, or 0.5.

39. B: The probability may be written as $P(E \text{ and } H) = P(E) \times P(H)$. Substituting the probability of each event gives $(E \text{ and } H) = \frac{1}{2} \times \frac{1}{2}$, which simplifies to $\frac{1}{4}$.

40. A: This situation describes a permutation, since order matters. The formula for calculating a combination is $P(n, r) = \frac{n!}{(n-r)!}$. This situation may be represented as $P(6,3) = \frac{6!}{(6-3)!}$, which equals 120.

41. A: The series is an infinite geometric series. The sum may be calculated using the formula $S = \frac{a}{1-r}$, where a represents the value of the first term and r represents the common ratio. Substituting 1 for a and $\frac{1}{2}$ for r gives $S = \frac{1}{1-\frac{1}{2}}$ or 2.

42. A: A Venn diagram such as the one shown below may be drawn to assist in finding the answer.

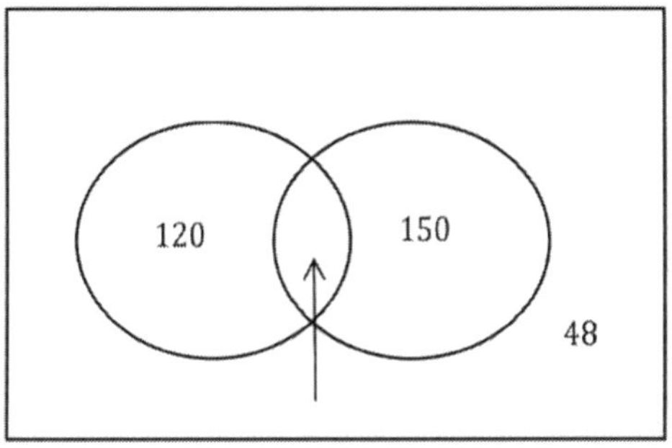

Since the set contains 320 total people, the solution is equal to $320 - (120 + 150 + 48)$ or 2 people.

43. D: The Pythagorean theorem may be used to find the diagonal distance from the top of his head to the base of the shadow. The following equation may be written and solved for c: $5.8^2 + 6.2^2 = c^2$. Thus, $c \approx 8.5$. The distance is approximately 8.5 ft.

44. D: The point $(5, -5)$ lies on the line segment that has a slope of -2 and passes through $(3, -1)$. If $(5, -5)$ is one of the endpoints of the line segment, then the other would be (1,3).

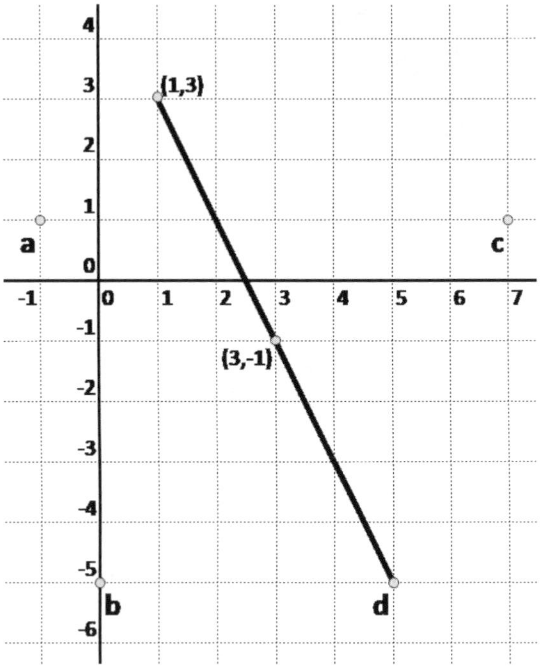

45. B: The mean is pulled towards the tail of a skewed distribution. It is not pulled towards the area with the larger frequency of scores. Outliers pull the mean towards those outliers.

46. C: Second. Ordinal numbers are first, second, third, fourth, etc.

47. B: This is a formative assessment because she is assessing students while she is still teaching the unit. Summative assessments are given at the end of the unit. Formal assessments are usually quizzes or tests. Informal assessments include asking individual students questions. Therefore, the correct choice is B.

48. B: A cube has six square faces. The arrangement of these faces in a two-dimensional figure is a net of a cube if the figure can be folded to form a cube. If choice B is folded, the bottom square in the second column will overlap the fourth square in the top row, so the figure does not represent a net of a cube. The other figures represent three of the eleven possible nets of a cube.

49. C: One strategy is to consider a progression of polygons with fewer sides and look for a pattern in the number of the polygons' diagonals.

Polygon	Sides	Diagonals	Additional Diagonals
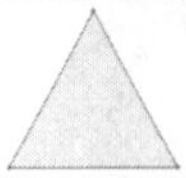	3	0	-
	4	2	2
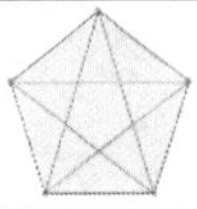	5	5	3
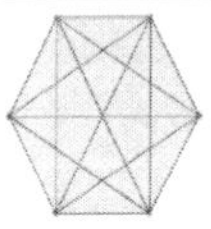	6	9	4

A quadrilateral has two more diagonals than a triangle, a pentagon has three more diagonals than a quadrilateral, and a hexagon has four more diagonals than a pentagon. Continue this pattern to find that a dodecagon has 54 diagonals.

50. A: $A \cap B$ means "A intersect B," or the elements that are common to both sets. "A intersect B" represents "A and B," that is, an element is in the intersection of A and B if it is in A *and* it is in B. The elements 2, 5, and 8 are common to both sets.

Science

1. B: When an astronomer observing stars detects a blue shift, he can conclude the star is moving closer or toward him. This is an example of the practical application of the Doppler effect in astronomy as applied to electromagnetic waves. The Doppler effect explains the change of wavelength caused by motion of the source or the relative difference in velocity between the observer and the source. When observing stars, a red shift or blue shift can be used to measure the speed that stars and galaxies are approaching or receding. Blue light has a higher frequency than red light. A red shift indicates a receding source.

2. C: A salt is a general term for the neutral ionic product of a neutralization reaction between an acid and a base. Often, table salt, or sodium chloride, is mistakenly characterized as "salt," indicating that all salts are this compound. Although it is very common for a salt to be composed of a metal and a nonmetal, this is not always true, as in the case of the salt ammonium chloride. The ammonium ion (NH_4^+) is a polyatomic ion composed of non-metals. Likewise, many salts are composed of an alkali or alkaline earth metal and a halogen, but this is not always the case.

3. B: Group 2 makes up the alkaline earth metals on the periodic chart of elements. There are 18 groups, or vertical columns, on the periodic table. In general, Group 2, alkaline earth metals, are characterized by silver colored, soft metals that melt at high temperatures. They also combine well with halogens to form salts and have two electrons in their valence level. Answer A, Group 1, are called the alkali metals or lithium family. Answer C, Group 13, is the boron family. Answer D, Group 17, are known as the halogens or fluorine family.

4. C: A laccolith is formed when an intrusion of magma injected between two layers of sedimentary rock forces the overlying strata upward to create a dome-like form. Eventually, the magma cools, the sedimentary rock wears away and the formation is exposed. Sills and dikes are both examples of sheet intrusions, where magma has inserted itself into other rock. Sills are horizontal and dikes are vertical. A caldera is a crater-like feature that was formed from the collapse of a volcano after erupting.

5. C: In order to pinpoint the exact location of the epicenter, seismograms are needed from three widely separate locations. A circle is drawn around each location with a radius equal to the distance of the earthquake. Since two circles can cross in two locations, a third circle is needed to pinpoint which intersection is the location of the epicenter. The intersection of the three circles is the location of the epicenter.

6. A: Orange red stars have temperatures less than 3,700 K. Yellow orange stars range between 3,700 and 5,200 K. Yellow white stars range between 5,200 and 6,000 K. Blue white stars range between 10,000 and 30,000 K.

7. A: Water actually has its lowest volume at four degrees Celsius. Water stops contracting at four degrees Celsius. Water expands as it cools from four degrees Celsius to zero degrees Celsius.

8. C: Exfoliation is a type of physical or mechanical weathering that occurs when rocks peel off in sheets or layers. No chemical change occurs. Oxidation, hydrolysis, and carbonation are all types of chemical weathering.

9. C: Clouds form when water in the air condenses onto condensation nuclei in the air. Atmospheric water vapor will condense when the atmospheric temperature reaches the dew point.

10. B: Anabolic processes are those that use energy to build larger molecules. In cells, adenosine triphosphate (ATP) is used as a source of energy. A condensation reaction joins two molecules together to make a larger molecule and, in the process, also produces a water molecule. Condensation reactions are important in protein synthesis. Anabolic processes are often reduction reactions. Catabolism breaks down molecules and usually generates energy. Catabolic reactions are often oxidation reactions. Hydrolysis is a catabolic process where water is added to a molecule and then split, resulting in the molecule breaking apart into two different molecules. Hydrolysis is the opposite of condensation.

11. B: Photosynthesis converts carbon dioxide into sugars that plants use. Three types are C3, C4, and CAM. C3 is used by most plants. C4 and CAM are used by desert plants. C4 first forms a four-carbon sugar instead of the three-carbon sugar formed by C3. Also, the stomata of C4 plants are faster at absorbing carbon dioxide and do not have to open as long, so less water is lost by transpiration. A C4 plant, such as saltbush, corn, or some grasses, would live in an arid environment rather than a moist, marine or dark environment. Plants that use the CAM (Crassulacean Acid Metabolism) type of photosynthesis also use water more efficiently as their stomata are closed during the day and open at night. Desert cacti are examples.

12. C: Translation is the process of the tRNA bringing the correct amino acid to the ribosome according to the sequence of the mRNA. Since translation only involves RNA, the four bases are adenine (A), cytosine (C), guanine (G), and uracil (U). There is no thymine (T) used in RNA. Cytosine (C) and guanine (G) pair and adenine (A) and uracil (U) pair. A codon is the triplet sequence that represents a specific amino acid or a start/stop point. It is on the messenger RNA (mRNA). The anticodon is on tRNA and corresponds to the amino acid used by the ribosome during translation.

They are complementary. UGC becomes AUG; AUG becomes CGA. The mRNA codon sequence is U G C A U G C G A if the anticodon sequence formed during translation is A C G U A C G C U.

13. C: The fraction of offspring that that have the genotype BbSs is $\frac{4}{16}$. A dihybrid cross considers two traits at a time, in this case, eye color and hair color. In the parent (P) generation, a parent with the genotype BBSS would be crossed with a parent with the genotype bbss. The offspring are considered the F1 generation and all would have the genotype BbSs. This question asks about the F2 generation, which is the offspring between a cross of the F1 generation. Therefore, the parent genotypes in this question would be BbSs. To solve, develop a Punnet square of 16 cells. Each parent will produce the following gametes: BS, Bs, bS, bs. Place these across the top and the side. After completing the square, the resulting offspring show that four would have the genotype BbSs.

P → F1

	BS
bs	BbSs

F1 → F2

	BS	**Bs**	**bS**	**bs**
BS	BBSS	BBSs	BbSS	BbSs
Bs	BBSs	BBss	BbSs	Bbss
bS	BbSS	BbSs	bbSS	bbSs
bs	BbSs	Bbss	bbSs	bbss

14. D: An inversion mutation is represented in the sequence 1 5 4 3 2 6. An inversion error is a type of mutation where an entire sequence of DNA is reversed. In this case, 2 3 4 5 has been reversed to 5 4 3 2. Answer A, breakage, in a gene can mess up its function entirely or lead to a translocation of genetic information. Answer B, deletion, is when a section of DNA is omitted or lost. Answer C, insertion, is when an extra base pair is added to a DNA sequence. Deletions and insertions can lead to a frameshift effect where entire sequences are thrown off because one nucleotide is wrong. This could result in coding for the wrong amino acid and non-functioning proteins.

15. B: Some RNA molecules in extant organisms have enzymatic activity; for example, the formation of peptide bonds on ribosomes is catalyzed by an RNA molecule. This and other information have led scientists to believe that the most likely molecules to first demonstrate enzymatic activity were RNA molecules.

16. A: Long-term energy storage in animals takes the form of fat. Animals also store energy as glycogen, and plants store energy as starch, but these substances are for shorter-term use. Fats are a good storage form for chemical energy because fatty acids bond to glycerol in a condensation reaction to form fats (triglycerides). This reaction, which releases water, allows for the compacting of high-energy fatty acids in a concentrated form.

17. C: Genes code for proteins, and genes are discrete lengths of DNA on chromosomes. An allele is a variant of a gene (different DNA sequence). In diploid organisms, there may be two versions of each gene.

18. C: Chloroplasts contain the light-absorbing compound chlorophyll, which is essential in photosynthesis. This gives leaves their green color. Chloroplasts also contain yellow and red carotenoid pigments, which give leaves red and yellow colors in the fall as chloroplasts lose their chlorophyll.

19. C: One way to measure the density of an irregularly shaped object is to submerge it in water and measure the displacement. This is done by taking the mass (40 grams), then finding the volume by measuring how much water it displaces. Fill a graduated cylinder with water and record the amount. Put the object in the water and record the water level. Subtract the difference in water levels to get the amount of water displaced, which is also the volume of the object. In this case, 4.5 liters minus 2.5 liters equals 2 liters. Divide mass by volume (40 grams divided by 2 liters) to get 20 g/L (grams per liter).

20. B: The refractive index is an optical property which is not related to the organization of the periodic table. Elements on the periodic table are arranged into periods, or rows, according to atomic number, which is the number of protons in the nucleus. The periodic table illustrates the recurrence of properties. Each column, or group, contains elements that share similar properties, such as reactivity.

21. C: Heat transfer can never occur from a cooler object to a warmer object. While the second law of thermodynamics implies that heat never spontaneously transfers from a cooler object to a warmer object, it is possible for heat to be transferred to a warmer object, given the proper input of work to the system. This is the principle by which a refrigerator operates. Work is done to the system to transfer heat from the objects inside the refrigerator to the air surrounding the refrigerator. All other answer choices are true.

22. A: Newton's first law (inertia) says an object in motion stays in motion, and an object at rest stays at rest, unless external forces act on them. Choice A is an excellent demonstration because it shows the ball at rest and in motion. At rest, the ball stays at rest until a force acts on it. When the ball is moving, there is no force acting on the ball in the direction of motion. Thus, the natural state of the ball is to be at rest or moving with a constant speed. Choice C is not a good demonstration because the force of friction is what makes it hard to move the heavy object. Choice B is a good demonstration of equilibrium and friction. Running a current through parallel wires (D) has nothing to do with Newton's first law.

23. B: Solubility is the amount of solute present in saturated solution. For a gas solute in a liquid solvent, increasing the temperature increases the kinetic energy of the gas molecules, which decreases the solubility of the gas in the liquid. Increasing the pressure of the gas increases the number of particles escaping from the surface and decreases the solubility. For a solid solute in a liquid solvent, increasing the temperature increases the kinetic energy, which increases the number of collisions and increases the solubility. Increasing the pressure of a solid solute in a liquid has little or no effect on solubility.

24. B: Pressure can be defined as force per unit area. This is evident from common pressure units such as lb/in^2 and N/m^2. Mass per unit volume is a description of density.

25. C: Acids react with metals like zinc to produce hydrogen gas. Acids turn litmus red, not blue. Acids donate protons, they do not accept them. Acids produce H^+ ions in aqueous solution, not OH^- ions.

26. D: In a homogeneous solution, the substance that is dissolved is the solute. A mixture of sugar and water is a homogenous solution in which the sugar is the solute, and the water is the solvent. A mixture of salt and water is a homogeneous solution in which the salt is the solute, and the water is the solvent. A mixture of ash in air is a description of smoke, which is a colloid. A mixture of salt and pepper is a heterogeneous mixture.

27. A: The period of a simple pendulum depends on the length and the rate of acceleration due to gravity. The period is independent of amplitude (to a good approximation) for amplitudes less than about 15 degrees. The period of a pendulum is unaffected by increasing the mass.

28. C: A chemical change involves a chemical reaction where new products are formed. When silver tarnishes, a thin layer of corrosion is formed, indicating a chemical change. A physical change does not produce new substances. Phase changes such as evaporation and sublimation are examples of physical changes. Salt dissolving in water is also a physical change because the ions just separate, and no new substances are formed.

29. C: Weighing the benefits to people and the economy against the risks is why governments would conduct a risk-benefit analysis before making decisions about city planning and development. Answer A, which states that governments must know what the benefits of a new development are for people and the economy in order to persuade opponents and the public who are against it, would be incorrect because the intention would be to build regardless of risk. Answer D, which suggests that the benefits to people and the economy can be used to ignore the risks associated with any new development, would also be incorrect as it would be unethical to ignore the risks.

30. A: This is an issue that would be regulated by the Food and Drug Administration (FDA), as it regulates the packaging of meat products, among many other types of food. Answer B would not be an issue for the FDA. The Environmental Protection Agency (EPA) regulates issues regarding the environment as well as Superfund cleanups. Neither answer C, about genetic engineering of humans, nor answer D, about cell use in industry, relate to food and drugs and would not fall under the jurisdiction of the FDA.

31. D: Sources of renewable energy include geothermal power, solar energy, and wind power. Sources of nonrenewable energy include nuclear power and fossil fuels like coal, natural gas, and crude oil.

32. A: Pros of wind energy include space efficiency, no pollution, and low operational costs. Cons of wind energy include wind fluctuation, threats to wildlife, and the expense to manufacture and install.

33. C: Repeating the experiment validates data. Each separate experiment is called a repetition. It should be possible to replicate the results of experiments or tests. Similar data gathered from many experiments can also be used to quantify the validity of the hypothesis. Repeating the experiments allows the student to observe variation in the results. Variation in data can be caused by a variety of errors or may be evidence against the hypothesis. Answer D, create a hypothesis, comes before experiments. Answer A, communicate the results, and B, draw a conclusion, occur after testing.

34. D: Once a hypothesis has been verified and accepted, it becomes a theory. A theory is a generally accepted explanation that has been highly developed and tested. A theory can explain data and be expected to predict outcomes of tests. A fact is considered to be an objective and verifiable observation, whereas a scientific theory is a greater body of accepted knowledge, principles, or relationships that might explain a fact. A law is an explanation of events for which the outcome is always the same. A conclusion is more of an opinion and could be based on observation, evidence, fact, laws, or even beliefs.

35. D: A good hypothesis must be testable. This means it may be proved or disproved by testing using a controlled experiment. A controlled experiment may have several constants but only one independent variable.

36. A: Observation includes collecting evidence, using the five senses, and writing descriptions. Classifying includes grouping items based on similarities, differences, and interrelationships. Inferring includes explaining or interpreting collected evidence. Communication is reporting to others what has been found by experimentation.

37. C: Plants growing on land depend on sunlight to perform photosynthesis, the process whereby they convert sunlight's energy to chemical energy as fuel for their life functions. Undersea plants (A) need water and nutrients like land plants; they do not need all gases in the atmosphere but need the gases in the water, and they need less light than land plants, or no light at all, to survive. Mammals (B) need air, water, and nutrients; some mammals need more or less light, but none need light for photosynthesis as land plants do. Humans (D) are also mammals.

38. D: Sedimentary rock is formed on the surface of the earth, deposited in layers as the result of natural processes like erosion. Igneous (A) rocks are formed from volcanic eruptions. Obsidian (B) is just one type of igneous rock. Metamorphic (C) rocks form deep in the earth's crust through heavy pressure and/or heat, which metamorphose or change sedimentary and igneous rocks far below the surface.

39. B: Newton's First law of motion states *both* that an object at rest tends to stay at rest (A), and an object in motion tends to stay in motion (C), unless or until an opposing force changes this. Newton's *Third law of motion* states that for every action there is an equal and opposite reaction (D).

40. C: The pressure decreases to one-third. A gas in a closed container at constant temperature will decrease in pressure to one-third when the volume of the container is tripled. The ideal gas law is $PV = nRT$ where P is pressure, V is volume, n is the moles of the gas, R is the gas constant, and T is temperature. Dividing by volume gives the following expression for pressure:

$$P = \frac{nRT}{V}$$

Boyle's Law indicates that pressure and volume are inversely proportional. The pressure cannot be increased because that would imply that pressure and volume are directly proportional.

41. C: Leeuwenhoek is considered to have been the father of microscopy. Pasteur discovered the role of microorganisms in disease. Koch determined that each disease has a specific pathogen. James Watson developed the science of genetics.

42. D: Exhaust fumes are an ever-present concern, while the others are incidents that might or might not occur. A combustion engine of any kind produces fumes which can rapidly cause health damage, brain damage, or death if allowed to fill an inadequately ventilated space. Therefore, activities of this kind are usually conducted near an open garage door or loading dock if not out-of-doors. A situation guaranteed to happen—the production of fumes—is of higher priority than incidental dangers.

43. D: An atom has a neutral charge if its atomic number is equal to its number of electrons. The atomic number (Z) of an element refers to the number of protons in the nucleus. If an atom has fewer or more electrons than its atomic number, then it will be positively or negatively charged, respectively. Cations are positively charged ions; anions are negatively charged ones.

44. D: Human beings, like other mammals, birds, fish, reptiles, and spiders, have simple life cycles in that they are either born live or hatched from eggs, and then grow to adulthood. Frogs (A), newts (B), and grasshoppers (C) undergo metamorphoses wherein their forms change. Frogs and newts are amphibians; they begin life underwater, breathing through gills, but breathe through lungs by adulthood and move from the water to live on the land. Grasshoppers hatch from eggs into larvae, wormlike juvenile forms that do most of the feeding they need; then they progress to adulthood.

45. C: For an experiment to be considered successful, it must yield data that others can reproduce. A reasonable hypothesis (A) may be considered part of a well-designed experiment. A well-written lab report (B) and computer-aided statistical analysis (D) may be considered part of an experiment that is reported on by individuals with expertise.

46. B: Work is defined as the force used to move a mass over a distance. The amount of energy used to accomplish a job is a non-scientific definition of work. The amount of energy used per unit of time is the definition of power. Energy stored in an object due to its position is the definition of potential energy.

47. B: Large buildings with visible exteriors made almost entirely of glass are often considered to be designed as such for aesthetic architectural purposes, although there are practical advantages. One of these is the insulating property of glass, a particularly useful aspect on very tall buildings, where the ambient outside temperatures and wind patterns are irregular and undesirable. Little support is provided by glass walls, so these buildings usually have a core of steel girders. Decoration is by definition not a practical purpose, nor does glass help issues of tenant privacy.

48. D: Refraction is the process whereby the speed of light is changed as it passes from one transparent medium, like air, to another, like water. The change in speed bends the light wave. Scattering (A) is the process whereby light bounces back at multiple angles when it strikes a rough or uneven surface (instead of bouncing back at a single angle as when it strikes a smooth surface). When light bounces back off a surface, this is reflection (C). Materials that do not reflect *any* light waves (smoothly or scattered) or refract any light waves appear opaque (i.e., we cannot see through them) because they take in all frequencies of light; this is absorption (B).

49. A: The stream of charged particles that escape the Sun's gravitational pull is called solar wind. Solar wind is composed primarily of protons and electrons, and these particles are deflected away from the Earth by its magnetic field. When stray particles do manage to enter the atmosphere, they cause the auroras (northern and southern lights) and geomagnetic storms that can affect power grids.

50. B: Ohm's Law states that voltage and current in an electrical circuit are directly proportional to one another. Ohm's Law can be expressed as $V = IR$, where V is voltage, I is current and R is resistance. Voltage is also known as electrical potential difference and is the force that moves electrons through a circuit. For a given amount of resistance, an increase in voltage will result in an increase in current. Resistance and current are inversely proportional to each other. For a given voltage, an increase in resistance will result in a decrease in current.

Social Studies

1. A: The Nile River flooded regularly and reliably, irrigating the crops of the ancient Egyptians. This best explains the stability of Egyptian culture. Answer B can be rejected because though the Nile River is expansive; its size did not prevent the Egyptian people from settling elsewhere. Answer C can be rejected because the Valley of the Kings, an ancient Egyptian city, did not separate Upper and Lower Egypt. Answer D can be rejected because, even if true, interaction with other cultures is more likely to lead to a dynamic, changing culture than a stable, unchanging culture.

2. D: Ziggurats were towers dedicated to gods; their prevalence indicates the importance of religion in Mesopotamian culture. The other options can be rejected because they pair accurate facts about Mesopotamia with inaccurate summaries of the purposes of the ziggurats. For example, while rulers of Mesopotamian cities fought among themselves, ziggurats were not used as lookouts. This eliminates option A. Although astrology was practiced in Mesopotamia, ziggurats did not function as places for stargazing or observing the sky. Finally, Mesopotamian cities were ruled by kings, but the ziggurats were not dedicated to them. This eliminates options B and C.

3. B: Although Charlemagne himself may not have believed his authority was conferred by the pope, Charlemagne's successors sometimes used the title "Holy Roman Emperor" (given to them by the pope) as a basis for their authority. Thus, the title "Holy Roman Emperor" strengthened the notion that political authority was conferred by the pope. Charlemagne united much of Europe under a single ruler prior to being named Holy Roman Emperor. While Catholicism may have been the recognized religion, the naming of Charlemagne as Holy Roman Emperor did not make it so. After being so named, Charlemagne did not renounce his conquests. This eliminates options A, C, and D respectively.

4. C: Under the Western European feudal system, rulers granted vassals land in exchange for military and political service. Although the right to use land would often pass from father to son, it was not on the basis of blood relations that a ruler granted land to a vassal; this eliminates option B. Religious institutions such as monasteries did indeed own land, but did not own most of it, eliminating option A. Finally, feudalism was a land-based economy that made a shift from a spice-based economy to a gold-based economy. Therefore, option D can be eliminated.

5. A: The Crusades' biggest impact upon Europe's Jewish population was that entire Jewish communities were killed during the First Crusade. This is the only option that accurately describes historical effects of the Crusades on the Jewish population. Rather than diminishing anti-Jewish sentiment, the Crusades seemed to inflame it, eliminating option B. One specific example of Crusades-era anti-Semitism is that many Jewish people were excluded from particular trades, and thus did not profit from the Crusades. This fact eliminates option C. Finally, there were no Jewish-only battalions during the Crusades, eliminating option D.

6. B: Johann Gutenberg's printing press led to increased scientific knowledge and advancement as scientific texts were printed and dispersed throughout Europe. Because the distribution of such texts extended outside of Germany, options C and D may be eliminated. Gutenberg Bibles were printed using Gutenberg's press, and thus Gutenberg's invention was likely a factor in the Reformation of the Catholic Church. In fact, Martin Luther's Ninety-Five Theses (against the Catholic Church) were printed using a printing press. However, this reformation occurred alongside, rather than in place of, the advancement of scientific knowledge. This eliminates option A.

7. D: The Triple Alliance allowed the city-states to conquer city-states and land by combining forces against mutual enemies. The Triple Alliance and its conquered areas are commonly thought of as the Aztec Empire. While some conquered areas did rebel against the Aztec Empire at the time the Spanish conquistadores arrived, such rebellion did not specifically concern the city-states of the Triple Alliance. Texcoco and Tlacopan did not use the Alliance as a front against Tenochtitlan. The Triple Alliance had nothing to do with the number of annual human sacrifices. This eliminates options A, B, and C.

8. A: The Catholic Church was both powerful and wealthy in medieval Europe. It affected the lives of both the rich and poor; for example, wealthy families often donated to monasteries in exchange for prayers on the donors' behalf. This eliminates option B. Because of these donations, some monasteries became quite wealthy. Rather than being a neutral force, the Catholic Church wielded political power. In medieval times, some claimed that rulers derived their authority to rule from the Catholic Church itself. These facts eliminate options C and D.

9. B: Akbar allowed the practice of both Hinduism and Islam, despite pressure from Islamic religious leaders to do otherwise. Akbar specifically permitted the construction of Hindu temples, which freed Akbar from Hindu resistance that he might otherwise have faced. This fact eliminates answer D. Breaking from some past practices, Akbar also used cash instead of land to pay empire officials, allowing him to control more land. Because of this, option A can be rejected. Option C can be rejected because Akbar allowed certain defeated princes to keep their lands.

10. A: In the 1780s, the French national debt was very high. The French nobility adamantly resisted attempts by King Louis XVI to reform tax laws, which led to a high tax burden on the French peasantry. The French government spent almost 50% of its national expenditures on debt-related payments during the 1780s; thus it could not and did not spend almost 60% to finance luxuries for the French nobility. This eliminates choice B. King Louis XVI temporarily banned the guild system to bolster, rather than stifle, free trade. Because this system gave skilled craftsmen economic advantages, journeymen opposed ending the system. This eliminates choice D. Regardless of the status of guilds before the French Revolution, French society did not offer many opportunities for upward social mobility. Few peasants were able to advance. This eliminates choice C.

11. D: The ancient Indus Valley civilization, also known in its mature phase as the Harappan civilization, existed in what now encompasses all of the listed countries today, except Turkey. This culture flourished from circa 2600–1900 BC, during the Bronze Age. This civilization included the most eastern portion of Balochistan in what is now Iran; the most western parts of what is now India; the majority of what is now Pakistan; and the southeastern part of Afghanistan.

12. B: Historians have determined that the Yellow River Valley in China began to develop into a cultural center during the Neolithic Era between c. 12,000–10,000 BC. The Shang Dynasty occurred between c. 1700–1046 BC—still part of the Ancient Era, but very long after the Neolithic era. The Xia Dynasty ruled between circa 2100–1600 BC, preceding the Shang Dynasty but still long after the Neolithic Era. Archaeological evidence exists of Homo erectus in China from more than a million years ago, during the Paleolithic Era, but the Yellow River Valley was not an emergent cultural center that long ago.

13. C: The increasing popularity of Thai food in the United States is an example of cultural convergence, or the intersection of traits or customs from two distinct cultures. Thailand's cuisine has been introduced to the United States, but it has undergone subtle changes as a result of the desires and practices of the American consumer. The phenomenon of cultural convergence is credited with much of the innovation in any society. Cultural divergence, on the other hand, is the practice of shielding one culture from the influence of another. France, for instance, seeks to limit the influence of American culture on its citizens. Assimilation is the process by which a minority group gradually adopts the culture of the majority group. For example, many Native Americans assimilated into the European-style culture of the early American settlers. Acculturation is the process of obtaining the practices and ideas of a culture. A child undergoes acculturation, wherein he or she learns to think and act appropriately for his or her setting.

14. C: The cycle of demographic transition is best illustrated by a line graph. Demographic transition is a phenomenon in which a region's growth rate increases rapidly, peaks, and then decreases slowly over a long time. In the early phase of a region's development, both the birth and death rates are high, which can cause the population to fluctuate. As the people of the region become settled, the growth rate calms down, and the region enters a period of rapid increase. Political maps are better at depicting borders and the locations of cities, while pie charts are better at representing proportions. Flow-line maps are good for illustrating the movement of people, goods, or trends across a physical area.

15. C: The first great human civilization was the Sumerian civilization, which was located in Mesopotamia. Mesopotamia encompasses the area between the Tigris and Euphrates Rivers in modern-day Iraq and is also referred to as "the Cradle of Civilization," and includes part of the Fertile Crescent.

The Sumerian civilization is credited with being the first to practice serious, year-round agriculture. There is question over whether Sumeria or Ancient Egypt was the first to have a written language. Sumeria's writing began hieroglyphically and then developed into a form of writing known as cuneiform.

16. A: Anubis was the Egyptian god of the dead, typically depicted as being half human and half jackal. Hatshepsut was an Egyptian queen who declared herself king while acting as regent for her stepson (who was also her son-in-law). She was the fifth pharaoh of Egypt's 18th dynasty. Ramesses (or Ramses) II was the third pharaoh of Egypt's 19th Dynasty, and Egypt's greatest, most powerful and most celebrated pharaoh. He is also traditionally considered to be the pharaoh of the Bible's Book of Exodus. His tomb in the Valley of the Kings was discovered in 1881. Tutankhamen was the boy pharaoh whose tomb was found in 1922, intact and untouched by tomb raiders, leading to a surge of popular interest in ancient Egypt.

17. C: Pope Urban II's plan for an army made up of previously trained military personnel was thwarted by the popular excitement concerning the First Crusade. This led to the creation of large armies primarily made up of untrained, unskilled, undisciplined, and ill- or unequipped soldiers, most of whom were recruited from the poorest levels of society. These armies were the first to set forth on the Crusade, which became known as the People's Crusade. Even though some of these armies contained knights, they were ultimately ineffective as fighting forces. These armies were prone to rioting and raiding surrounding areas for food and supplies and were viewed as a destabilizing influence by local leaders. They were defeated in battle and many converted to Islam to avoid being killed.

18. D: Despite the growing amount of literacy in the 1500s, due principally to the invention of the printing press and the availability of texts, the majority of Europeans remained illiterate.

19. B: In 1792, when the French Revolution turned into European war, American traders conducted business with both sides. It is not true that Washington allied with the French at this time. Washington issued a Proclamation of Neutrality in 1792 when the French went to war with

European countries. While they did trade with both sides, American merchants profited the most from the French West Indies, not the British West Indies. The Spanish navy did not retaliate against America for trading with the French. Though Spain was an ally of Britain, it was the British who most often seized American ships and forced their crews to serve the British navy. Edmond-Charles Genêt, or Citizen Genêt, a French ambassador to the United States during the French Revolution, defied Washington's policy of neutrality by encouraging the American people to support the French. Washington was embarrassed by this violation. He did not agree with it.

20. D: After the two major Italian banks collapsed, wealthy investors who would normally have reinvested their disposable income did not do this, since the economy did not favor it. Instead, they invested their money in artistic and cultural products. After the Black Death killed a third of Europe's population, the survivors were mainly upper classes with more money to spend on art, architecture, and other luxuries. The plague deaths also resulted in a labor shortage, thereby creating more work opportunities for the surviving people in lower classes. As a result, these survivors' positions in society appreciated. Once plague deaths subsided and population growth in Europe began to reassert itself, a greater demand existed for products and services. At the same time, the number of people available to provide these products and services was still smaller than in the past. Consequently, more merchants, artisans, and bankers emerged in order to provide the services and products people wanted, thereby creating a class of citizens between the lower-class laborers and the upper-class elite.

21. C: The Sugar Act of 1764 raised import duties on goods which were not of British origin, including sugar, while reducing the import tax on molasses. The Stamp Act of 1765 was a tax of paper and printed products, intended to help the British government recoup some of the costs of the French and Indian War. It was extremely unpopular with the colonists and was repealed in 1766. Lead was one of the goods taxed under the Townshend Acts, enacted in 1767, but it did not receive its own specific tax act. The Tea Act of 1773 was another unpopular tax and led to tea boycotts and was the catalyst for the Boston Tea Party.

22. B: The Founding Fathers decided that because the colonies did not have the right to elect members of Parliament, Parliament should not pass laws for them. The Declaration of Independence recognized the British Empire's government as being headed by the King of England, under whom the various local parliaments and legislative bodies served to enact laws for the peoples whom they represented. By addressing their ills to the king, the Founding Fathers sought to prevent the appearance that they acknowledged the British Parliament in London as having any authority over the American colonies.

23. B: *Marbury v. Madison* started with the election of Thomas Jefferson as third President of the United States. The lame-duck Congress responded by issuing a large number of judicial patents, which the incoming president and Secretary of State refused to deliver to their holders. Marbury, who was to receive a patent as Justice of the Peace, sued to demand delivery. What makes this case important is the decision which declared the judiciary's ability to overturn legislation that conflicted with the Constitution. The case states:

"It is emphatically the province and duty of the judicial department to say what the law is. Those who apply the rule to particular cases must, of necessity, expound and interpret that rule. If two laws conflict with each other, the courts must decide on the operation of each.

"So if a law be in opposition to the Constitution; if both the law and the constitution apply to a particular case, so that the court must either decide that case conformably to the law, disregarding the Constitution; or conformably to the Constitution, disregarding the law; the court must determine which of these conflicting rules governs the case. This is of the very essence of judicial duty.

"If, then, the courts are to regard the Constitution, and the Constitution is superior to any ordinary act of the legislature, the Constitution, and not such ordinary act, must govern the case to which they both apply."

Later, the ruling states: "The judicial power of the United States is extended to all cases arising under the Constitution." It was in this way that the Supreme Court achieved its now traditional ability to strike down laws and to act as the final arbitrator of what is and is not allowed under the US Constitution.

24. D: Abraham Lincoln issued the Thanksgiving Proclamation on October 3, 1863, in which he specified the last Thursday of November as a day of thanksgiving. The last Thursday in November was the traditional date for the Thanksgiving holiday for the next 76 years.

In 1939, President Roosevelt tried to change the holiday's date from the last Thursday in November to the second to last Thursday in November in order to stimulate the economy by creating a longer Christmas shopping season. This action met with resistance in some parts of the country, and a compromise was reached in 1941, setting the date of Thanksgiving as the fourth Thursday in November.

25. C: While wounds from war most certainly killed more than a few, European disease laid waste to vast swaths of Native American people who had no immunity to the foreign diseases which the Europeans carried. The forced marches took place in the mid-19th century under Andrew Jackson's presidency and are thus removed from the time frame in question.

26. A: The US Constitution, Article I, Section 3 states that: "The Senate of the United States shall be composed of two Senators from each state, chosen by the legislature thereof, for six years; and each Senator shall have one vote." This was the practice until the Seventeenth Amendment was ratified on April 8, 1913. The Seventeenth Amendment states that US Senators are to be elected by the people of the states which they serve and that the state executive branches may appoint replacement Senators if a Senate seat becomes vacant mid-term, until the state legislature can arrange for a popular election.

27. B: The Erie Canal opened in 1825 and created a water route between the Hudson River and Lake Erie. Water routes have historically been cheaper and easier than overland ones and the Erie Canal was originally proposed in the 1700s as a means of providing a shipping route to assist in settling the areas west of the Appalachian Mountains. The Mississippi River is to the west of the Great Lakes; its source is in Minnesota and it discharges into the Gulf of Mexico approximately 100 miles downstream of New Orleans, Louisiana. The Susquehanna River runs through New York, Pennsylvania, and Maryland and is the home of Three Mile Island, the site of the United States' largest nuclear disaster. The Lehigh River is located in eastern Pennsylvania.

28. C: The telegraph was a gigantic leap forward in the realm of communications. Before the telegraph, messages could take days, weeks, or months to reach their intended recipient, based upon the distance that they had to travel. The telegraph allowed people to send messages through use of electric signals transmitted over telegraph wires, allowing for instantaneous communications. The main drawbacks to the telegraph included the need to "translate" the message into and out of the appropriate telegraphic code and that the telegraph could only relay one message at a time. In contrast, the telephone allowed for spoken communication between people at different locations, increasing the efficiency and speed as the people on each end of the conversation could communicate multiple messages quickly and in one telephone conversation.

29. B: Sacagawea acted as Lewis and Clark's guide during their exploration of the Louisiana Purchase. She had been separated from her family at a young age and was reunited with her brother on the course of the expedition. Pocahontas was the daughter of Powhatan, the leader of the Algonquian tribes at the beginning of the 17th Century when the colony of Jamestown was founded in modern-day Virginia. Squanto's actual name was Tisquantum. He was the Native American who helped the Pilgrims after their first winter in Massachusetts. Wauwatosa is a suburb of Milwaukee, Wisconsin.

30. A: Lyndon Johnson became president following the assassination of John F. Kennedy on November 22, 1963. The Great Society was a series of social programs implemented under the direction of Lyndon Johnson. The Great Society's goal was to eliminate poverty and racial injustice in America. The Great Society began with economic reforms including a tax cut and the creation of the Office of Economic Opportunity. From there, it grew to include the enacting of laws creating the Medicare and Medicaid systems to assist the elderly and poor with their health care costs, respectively. Educational and Housing reforms followed.

31. A: James Madison, John Jay, and Alexander Hamilton published *The Federalist* in the *Independent Journal* and other publications in New York. It was a response to the Anti-Federalists in New York, who were slow to ratify the Constitution because they feared it gave the central government too much authority.

32. A: The Iroquois Confederacy was a confederacy of originally five (and later six) Native American Tribes, founded in 1570. Many decisions involved compromise between two sets of Lords from different tribes, analogous to the compromise involved in decision-making between the US House of Representatives and the US Senate. For the Confederacy to accept a decision, Mohawk and Seneca Lords needed to come to an agreement with Oneida and Cayuga Lords. Option B can be rejected because there is no chief in the Iroquois Confederacy analogous to the US President. Option C can be rejected because the Iroquois Confederacy did not involve representation based upon a tribe's population. Option D can be rejected because there was no judicial branch in the Iroquois Confederacy analogous to that of the US government.

33. C: The Federalist Party advocated a pro-British foreign policy and therefore opposed the War of 1812. This made the Federalists unpopular with many Americans; this unpopularity deepened when the war ended after several American victories. The Federalist Party did advocate a strong central government; however, this position was not a key factor in the Party's decline. This eliminates option D. Option A can be rejected because the Federalist Party did organize state political parties in states such as Connecticut, Delaware, and Maryland. Many members of the Federalist Party were pro-trade and pro-business, as many members were well-to-do businessmen. This eliminates option B.

34. D: After the American Revolution, the framers of the American government were concerned that a strong central government could lead to abuses of power. Accordingly, The Articles of Confederation did not grant the federal government the ability to raise taxes. Another restriction was the inability to regulate interstate commerce. Options A, B, and C can all be eliminated because, though the federal government was generally weak under the Articles of Confederation, the Articles granted the federal government each of the powers given in those options.

35. A: The citizens usually elect members of the local government such as mayors and city council. However, the state grants local governments their authority. State and local governments work independently and do not share authority the way the federal and state governments share power.

36. D: Keynes was an influential advocate of government intervention in a domestic economy for the purpose of stimulating economic growth. Keynes believed that appropriate government action could help end a recession more quickly; such measures might involve deficit spending. Because of this, and because Keynes is not associated with the view that deficit spending leads to inflation, option A can be eliminated. Additionally, Keynes is not closely associated with advocating government action to break up monopolies; this eliminates option B. Finally, option C can be eliminated because it describes Say's Law, which is in fact the opposite of Keynes's law: demand creates its own supply.

37. B: Economists understand the true cost of an action as not only its monetary cost but the cost of other opportunities missed as a result of pursuing that action. For example, if a person chooses to go to school rather than working, the cost of the action involves not only tuition and other associated fees and expenses, but the money one would have earned working, as well as the time one could have spent pursuing other activities. The concept of opportunity cost is not described by options A, C, or D, each of which is concerned only with monetary costs. Each of these answers can be rejected on that basis.

38. A: The production possibilities frontier shows the different possible combinations of goods (and/or services) a society can produce. If all other factors are even, producing more of Good A leads to a decreased production of Good B. If the PPF moves outward, that means a change in the factors of production that allows the economy to produce more goods—economic growth—has occurred. Something like innovation is an example of a cause of economic growth.

39. A: The input and output data illustrates the Law of Diminishing Marginal Returns, which states that as inputs are added during production, there eventually comes a time when increased inputs coincide with a decrease in marginal return.

40. A: GDP (Gross Domestic Product) is restricted to value produced within borders, whereas GNP (Gross National Product) is focused on value produced by companies regardless of borders.

41. B: Reification is the act of treating an abstraction as a real, concrete thing. For example, the concept of society might be useful, but it is not an actual, concrete thing separate from the components (such as people and infrastructure) that make up society. Options A, C, and D can all be rejected because none accurately capture the concept of reification. Social scientists might indeed be concerned with relative appropriateness of qualitative data and quantitative data, but using one over the other is not reification. Social scientists might use heuristic devices, but this is not simply reification (not all cases of reification are cases of using heuristic devices). Reification is not mistaking subjectivity for objectivity.

42. C: Learning such an association is classical conditioning. Generally, classical conditioning is the process of learning an association between two stimuli, one of which is neutral (in this instance, the sound of the can opener) and one to which an organism responds automatically (in this instance, food). Habituation occurs when an organism becomes desensitized to a repeated stimulus; this eliminates option B. Operant conditioning differs from classical conditioning in that, in the former, an organism changes its behavior in response to reinforcement (that is, an organism can change the outcome of an event by changing its behavior). This eliminates option A. Conformity is the process by which an organism changes its behavior to match others' behavior. This eliminates option D.

43. D: Race is the correct answer because it is not one of Max Weber's independent factors which form the basis for his theory of stratification. Social class, personal power, and social status are all incorrect because they are among Weber's independent factors forming his theory of stratification.

44. B: The philosophy of history is concerned with the ultimate significance of history as a field of study and asks questions concerning how history should be studied, including what social unit is correct to use when studying history—whether it is more important to look at the individual lives of ordinary people or to concentrate on the so-called big picture, looking at the overall trends in a society or culture; only giving personal treatment to people, such as George Washington, who had particular significance to the events surrounding them. The philosophy of history also looks for broad historical trends and progress.

45. A: Bias is a form of prejudice, and a historical work is considered biased when it is unreasonably shaped by the author's personal or institutional prejudices. It is wise for a teacher to choose material that comes from reputable sources and to verify that all material used in classroom presentations is reliable and appropriate. As long as the teacher is willing to do these things and show a variety of historical opinions, this is not an example of bias.

46. D: Federalists who helped frame the Constitution believed the central government needed to be stronger than what was established under the Articles of Confederation. Anti-federalists were against this and feared a strong federal government. A system of checks and balances was established to prevent the central government from taking too much power.

47. B: Maslow conceived of human needs in a hierarchy, and visualized this hierarchy as a pyramid. At the base of this pyramid are physiological needs, which are the most fundamental. Above these are security (C) needs such as shelter and a safe environment. Above these are social needs like feeling loved and belonging to a group. Above these are esteem (D) needs like feeling personal value, social recognition, and accomplishment. At the top of the pyramid are self-actualizing (A) needs, i.e. realizing one's full potential and attaining optimal personal growth. Maslow theorized that lower levels of need must be met before any higher level(s) can be addressed; hence physiological needs must be met first.

48. B: Oligarchy is defined as the rule by few. An example is aristocracy, which in ancient Greece, was government by an elite group of citizens as opposed to a monarchy. In later times, it meant government by the class of aristocrats, a privileged group, as opposed to democracy. The rule of one is called autocracy. Examples include monarchy, dictatorship, and many others. The rule by law is called a republic. Some examples are constitutional republics, parliamentary republics, and federal republics. The rule by many could apply to democracy, which governs according to the people's votes or to the collective leadership form of socialism, where no one individual has too much power.

49. C: Mercantilism is the economic theory that nations advance the goal of accumulating capital by maintaining a balance of trade such that the value of exports exceeds that of imports. Great Britain maintained colonies to provide an inexpensive source of raw materials while creating markets for the goods manufactured in England. Under free trade, governments refrain from hindering the international exchange of goods and services. Nations that are granted most favored nation status are assured of enjoying equal advantages in international trade. A laissez-faire capitalist economy would theoretically be completely free of government regulation.

50. B: The House has strict rules that limit debate. A filibuster can only occur in the Senate where senators can speak on topics other than the bill at hand and introduce amendments. A filibuster can be ended by a supermajority vote of 60 senators.

How to Overcome Test Anxiety

Just the thought of taking a test is enough to make most people a little nervous. A test is an important event that can have a long-term impact on your future, so it's important to take it seriously and it's natural to feel anxious about performing well. But just because anxiety is normal, that doesn't mean that it's helpful in test taking, or that you should simply accept it as part of your life. Anxiety can have a variety of effects. These effects can be mild, like making you feel slightly nervous, or severe, like blocking your ability to focus or remember even a simple detail.

If you experience test anxiety—whether severe or mild—it's important to know how to beat it. To discover this, first you need to understand what causes test anxiety.

Causes of Test Anxiety

While we often think of anxiety as an uncontrollable emotional state, it can actually be caused by simple, practical things. One of the most common causes of test anxiety is that a person does not feel adequately prepared for their test. This feeling can be the result of many different issues such as poor study habits or lack of organization, but the most common culprit is time management. Starting to study too late, failing to organize your study time to cover all of the material, or being distracted while you study will mean that you're not well prepared for the test. This may lead to cramming the night before, which will cause you to be physically and mentally exhausted for the test. Poor time management also contributes to feelings of stress, fear, and hopelessness as you realize you are not well prepared but don't know what to do about it.

Other times, test anxiety is not related to your preparation for the test but comes from unresolved fear. This may be a past failure on a test, or poor performance on tests in general. It may come from comparing yourself to others who seem to be performing better or from the stress of living up to expectations. Anxiety may be driven by fears of the future—how failure on this test would affect your educational and career goals. These fears are often completely irrational, but they can still negatively impact your test performance.

Elements of Test Anxiety

As mentioned earlier, test anxiety is considered to be an emotional state, but it has physical and mental components as well. Sometimes you may not even realize that you are suffering from test anxiety until you notice the physical symptoms. These can include trembling hands, rapid heartbeat, sweating, nausea, and tense muscles. Extreme anxiety may lead to fainting or vomiting. Obviously, any of these symptoms can have a negative impact on testing. It is important to recognize them as soon as they begin to occur so that you can address the problem before it damages your performance.

The mental components of test anxiety include trouble focusing and inability to remember learned information. During a test, your mind is on high alert, which can help you recall information and stay focused for an extended period of time. However, anxiety interferes with your mind's natural processes, causing you to blank out, even on the questions you know well. The strain of testing during anxiety makes it difficult to stay focused, especially on a test that may take several hours. Extreme anxiety can take a huge mental toll, making it difficult not only to recall test information but even to understand the test questions or pull your thoughts together.

Effects of Test Anxiety

Test anxiety is like a disease—if left untreated, it will get progressively worse. Anxiety leads to poor performance, and this reinforces the feelings of fear and failure, which in turn lead to poor performances on subsequent tests. It can grow from a mild nervousness to a crippling condition. If allowed to progress, test anxiety can have a big impact on your schooling, and consequently on your future.

Test anxiety can spread to other parts of your life. Anxiety on tests can become anxiety in any stressful situation, and blanking on a test can turn into panicking in a job situation. But fortunately, you don't have to let anxiety rule your testing and determine your grades. There are a number of relatively simple steps you can take to move past anxiety and function normally on a test and in the rest of life.

Physical Steps for Beating Test Anxiety

While test anxiety is a serious problem, the good news is that it can be overcome. It doesn't have to control your ability to think and remember information. While it may take time, you can begin taking steps today to beat anxiety.

Just as your first hint that you may be struggling with anxiety comes from the physical symptoms, the first step to treating it is also physical. Rest is crucial for having a clear, strong mind. If you are tired, it is much easier to give in to anxiety. But if you establish good sleep habits, your body and mind will be ready to perform optimally, without the strain of exhaustion. Additionally, sleeping well helps you to retain information better, so you're more likely to recall the answers when you see the test questions.

Getting good sleep means more than going to bed on time. It's important to allow your brain time to relax. Take study breaks from time to time so it doesn't get overworked, and don't study right before bed. Take time to rest your mind before trying to rest your body, or you may find it difficult to fall asleep.

Along with sleep, other aspects of physical health are important in preparing for a test. Good nutrition is vital for good brain function. Sugary foods and drinks may give a burst of energy but this burst is followed by a crash, both physically and emotionally. Instead, fuel your body with protein and vitamin-rich foods.

Also, drink plenty of water. Dehydration can lead to headaches and exhaustion, especially if your brain is already under stress from the rigors of the test. Particularly if your test is a long one, drink water during the breaks. And if possible, take an energy-boosting snack to eat between sections.

Along with sleep and diet, a third important part of physical health is exercise. Maintaining a steady workout schedule is helpful, but even taking 5-minute study breaks to walk can help get your blood pumping faster and clear your head. Exercise also releases endorphins, which contribute to a positive feeling and can help combat test anxiety.

When you nurture your physical health, you are also contributing to your mental health. If your body is healthy, your mind is much more likely to be healthy as well. So take time to rest, nourish your body with healthy food and water, and get moving as much as possible. Taking these physical steps will make you stronger and more able to take the mental steps necessary to overcome test anxiety.

Mental Steps for Beating Test Anxiety

Working on the mental side of test anxiety can be more challenging, but as with the physical side, there are clear steps you can take to overcome it. As mentioned earlier, test anxiety often stems from lack of preparation, so the obvious solution is to prepare for the test. Effective studying may be the most important weapon you have for beating test anxiety, but you can and should employ several other mental tools to combat fear.

First, boost your confidence by reminding yourself of past success—tests or projects that you aced. If you're putting as much effort into preparing for this test as you did for those, there's no reason you should expect to fail here. Work hard to prepare; then trust your preparation.

Second, surround yourself with encouraging people. It can be helpful to find a study group, but be sure that the people you're around will encourage a positive attitude. If you spend time with others who are anxious or cynical, this will only contribute to your own anxiety. Look for others who are motivated to study hard from a desire to succeed, not from a fear of failure.

Third, reward yourself. A test is physically and mentally tiring, even without anxiety, and it can be helpful to have something to look forward to. Plan an activity following the test, regardless of the outcome, such as going to a movie or getting ice cream.

When you are taking the test, if you find yourself beginning to feel anxious, remind yourself that you know the material. Visualize successfully completing the test. Then take a few deep, relaxing breaths and return to it. Work through the questions carefully but with confidence, knowing that you are capable of succeeding.

Developing a healthy mental approach to test taking will also aid in other areas of life. Test anxiety affects more than just the actual test—it can be damaging to your mental health and even contribute to depression. It's important to beat test anxiety before it becomes a problem for more than testing.

Study Strategy

Being prepared for the test is necessary to combat anxiety, but what does being prepared look like? You may study for hours on end and still not feel prepared. What you need is a strategy for test prep. The next few pages outline our recommended steps to help you plan out and conquer the challenge of preparation.

Step 1: Scope Out the Test

Learn everything you can about the format (multiple choice, essay, etc.) and what will be on the test. Gather any study materials, course outlines, or sample exams that may be available. Not only will this help you to prepare, but knowing what to expect can help to alleviate test anxiety.

Step 2: Map Out the Material

Look through the textbook or study guide and make note of how many chapters or sections it has. Then divide these over the time you have. For example, if a book has 15 chapters and you have five days to study, you need to cover three chapters each day. Even better, if you have the time, leave an extra day at the end for overall review after you have gone through the material in depth.

If time is limited, you may need to prioritize the material. Look through it and make note of which sections you think you already have a good grasp on, and which need review. While you are studying, skim quickly through the familiar sections and take more time on the challenging parts.

Write out your plan so you don't get lost as you go. Having a written plan also helps you feel more in control of the study, so anxiety is less likely to arise from feeling overwhelmed at the amount to cover.

Step 3: Gather Your Tools

Decide what study method works best for you. Do you prefer to highlight in the book as you study and then go back over the highlighted portions? Or do you type out notes of the important information? Or is it helpful to make flashcards that you can carry with you? Assemble the pens, index cards, highlighters, post-it notes, and any other materials you may need so you won't be distracted by getting up to find things while you study.

If you're having a hard time retaining the information or organizing your notes, experiment with different methods. For example, try color-coding by subject with colored pens, highlighters, or post-it notes. If you learn better by hearing, try recording yourself reading your notes so you can listen while in the car, working out, or simply sitting at your desk. Ask a friend to quiz you from your flashcards, or try teaching someone the material to solidify it in your mind.

Step 4: Create Your Environment

It's important to avoid distractions while you study. This includes both the obvious distractions like visitors and the subtle distractions like an uncomfortable chair (or a too-comfortable couch that makes you want to fall asleep). Set up the best study environment possible: good lighting and a comfortable work area. If background music helps you focus, you may want to turn it on, but otherwise keep the room quiet. If you are using a computer to take notes, be sure you don't have any other windows open, especially applications like social media, games, or anything else that could distract you. Silence your phone and turn off notifications. Be sure to keep water close by so you stay hydrated while you study (but avoid unhealthy drinks and snacks).

Also, take into account the best time of day to study. Are you freshest first thing in the morning? Try to set aside some time then to work through the material. Is your mind clearer in the afternoon or evening? Schedule your study session then. Another method is to study at the same time of day that you will take the test, so that your brain gets used to working on the material at that time and will be ready to focus at test time.

Step 5: Study!

Once you have done all the study preparation, it's time to settle into the actual studying. Sit down, take a few moments to settle your mind so you can focus, and begin to follow your study plan. Don't give in to distractions or let yourself procrastinate. This is your time to prepare so you'll be ready to fearlessly approach the test. Make the most of the time and stay focused.

Of course, you don't want to burn out. If you study too long you may find that you're not retaining the information very well. Take regular study breaks. For example, taking five minutes out of every hour to walk briskly, breathing deeply and swinging your arms, can help your mind stay fresh.

As you get to the end of each chapter or section, it's a good idea to do a quick review. Remind yourself of what you learned and work on any difficult parts. When you feel that you've mastered the material, move on to the next part. At the end of your study session, briefly skim through your notes again.

But while review is helpful, cramming last minute is NOT. If at all possible, work ahead so that you won't need to fit all your study into the last day. Cramming overloads your brain with more information than it can process and retain, and your tired mind may struggle to recall even previously learned information when it is overwhelmed with last-minute study. Also, the urgent nature of cramming and the stress placed on your brain contribute to anxiety. You'll be more likely to go to the test feeling unprepared and having trouble thinking clearly.

So don't cram, and don't stay up late before the test, even just to review your notes at a leisurely pace. Your brain needs rest more than it needs to go over the information again. In fact, plan to finish your studies by noon or early afternoon the day before the test. Give your brain the rest of the day to relax or focus on other things, and get a good night's sleep. Then you will be fresh for the test and better able to recall what you've studied.

Step 6: Take a Practice Test

Many courses offer sample tests, either online or in the study materials. This is an excellent resource to check whether you have mastered the material, as well as to prepare for the test format and environment.

Check the test format ahead of time: the number of questions, the type (multiple choice, free response, etc.), and the time limit. Then create a plan for working through them. For example, if you have 30 minutes to take a 60-question test, your limit is 30 seconds per question. Spend less time on the questions you know well so that you can take more time on the difficult ones.

If you have time to take several practice tests, take the first one open book, with no time limit. Work through the questions at your own pace and make sure you fully understand them. Gradually work up to taking a test under test conditions: sit at a desk with all study materials put away and set a timer. Pace yourself to make sure you finish the test with time to spare and go back to check your answers if you have time.

After each test, check your answers. On the questions you missed, be sure you understand why you missed them. Did you misread the question (tests can use tricky wording)? Did you forget the information? Or was it something you hadn't learned? Go back and study any shaky areas that the practice tests reveal.

Taking these tests not only helps with your grade, but also aids in combating test anxiety. If you're already used to the test conditions, you're less likely to worry about it, and working through tests until you're scoring well gives you a confidence boost. Go through the practice tests until you feel comfortable, and then you can go into the test knowing that you're ready for it.

Test Tips

On test day, you should be confident, knowing that you've prepared well and are ready to answer the questions. But aside from preparation, there are several test day strategies you can employ to maximize your performance.

First, as stated before, get a good night's sleep the night before the test (and for several nights before that, if possible). Go into the test with a fresh, alert mind rather than staying up late to study.

Try not to change too much about your normal routine on the day of the test. It's important to eat a nutritious breakfast, but if you normally don't eat breakfast at all, consider eating just a protein bar. If you're a coffee drinker, go ahead and have your normal coffee. Just make sure you time it so that the caffeine doesn't wear off right in the middle of your test. Avoid sugary beverages, and drink enough water to stay hydrated but not so much that you need a restroom break 10 minutes into the test. If your test isn't first thing in the morning, consider going for a walk or doing a light workout before the test to get your blood flowing.

Allow yourself enough time to get ready, and leave for the test with plenty of time to spare so you won't have the anxiety of scrambling to arrive in time. Another reason to be early is to select a good seat. It's helpful to sit away from doors and windows, which can be distracting. Find a good seat, get out your supplies, and settle your mind before the test begins.

When the test begins, start by going over the instructions carefully, even if you already know what to expect. Make sure you avoid any careless mistakes by following the directions.

Then begin working through the questions, pacing yourself as you've practiced. If you're not sure on an answer, don't spend too much time on it, and don't let it shake your confidence. Either skip it and come back later, or eliminate as many wrong answers as possible and guess among the remaining ones. Don't dwell on these questions as you continue—put them out of your mind and focus on what lies ahead.

Be sure to read all of the answer choices, even if you're sure the first one is the right answer. Sometimes you'll find a better one if you keep reading. But don't second-guess yourself if you do immediately know the answer. Your gut instinct is usually right. Don't let test anxiety rob you of the information you know.

If you have time at the end of the test (and if the test format allows), go back and review your answers. Be cautious about changing any, since your first instinct tends to be correct, but make sure you didn't misread any of the questions or accidentally mark the wrong answer choice. Look over any you skipped and make an educated guess.

At the end, leave the test feeling confident. You've done your best, so don't waste time worrying about your performance or wishing you could change anything. Instead, celebrate the successful completion of this test. And finally, use this test to learn how to deal with anxiety even better next time.

Review Video: Test Anxiety
Visit mometrix.com/academy and enter code: 100340

Important Qualification

Not all anxiety is created equal. If your test anxiety is causing major issues in your life beyond the classroom or testing center, or if you are experiencing troubling physical symptoms related to your anxiety, it may be a sign of a serious physiological or psychological condition. If this sounds like your situation, we strongly encourage you to seek professional help.

Additional Bonus Material

Due to our efforts to try to keep this book to a manageable length, we've created a link that will give you access to all of your additional bonus material:

mometrix.com/bonus948/megaeemc073074